Social Issues
in Literature

Race in Ralph Ellison's
Invisible Man

Other Books in the Social Issues in Literature Series:

Social Issues in Literature

Race in Ralph Ellison's *Invisible Man*

Hayley Mitchell Haugen, Book Editor

GREENHAVEN PRESS
A part of Gale, Cengage Learning

GALE
CENGAGE Learning

Detroit • New York • San Francisco • New Haven, Conn • Waterville, Maine • London

Elizabeth Des Chenes, *Managing Editor*

© 2012 Greenhaven Press, a part of Gale, Cengage Learning

Gale and Greenhaven Press are registered trademarks used herein under license.

For more information, contact:
Greenhaven Press
27500 Drake Rd.
Farmington Hills, MI 48331-3535
Or you can visit our Internet site at gale.cengage.com

For product information and technology assistance, contact us at

Gale Customer Support, 1-800-877-4253
For permission to use material from this text or product, submit all requests online at www.cengage.com/permissions

Further permissions questions can be emailed to permissionrequest@cengage.com

Articles in Greenhaven Press anthologies are often edited for length to meet page requirements. In addition, original titles of these works are changed to clearly present the main thesis and to explicitly indicate the author's opinion. Every effort is made to ensure that Greenhaven Press accurately reflects the original intent of the authors. Every effort has been made to trace the owners of copyrighted material.

Cover photograph copyright © Everett Collection Inc./Alamy

LIBRARY OF CONGRESS CATALOGING-IN-PUBLICATION DATA

Race in Ralph Ellison's Invisible man / Hayley Mitchell Haugen, book editor.
      p. cm. -- (Social issues in literature)
  Includes bibliographical references and index.
    ISBN 978-0-7377-5811-5 (hardcover) -- ISBN 978-0-7377-5812-2 (pbk.)
  1. Racism--United States. 2. Ellison, Ralph. 3. Social problems in literature. I.
Haugen, Hayley Mitchell, 1968-
    E185.615.R2126 2011
    305.800973--dc23
                                                                    2011023876

Printed in the United States of America
2 3 4 5 6   18 17 16 15 14

Contents

Despite changes in America's social and political climate since the publication of *Invisible Man*, Ellison's novel is still relevant decades later. Its satirical targets remain: racial prejudice, blind and deceptive leadership, and the betrayal of America's promise.

Invisible Man's relation to the radicalism of Ellison's youth is the source of its definition of an alternative basis for the African American social struggle after the Brotherhood experience, its continuing affirmation of possibilities of social reform, and its forecast of the actual content of the civil rights movement to come.

The ways in which black characters cope with inequity provide the situations of many African American novels, a genre that frequently relies on Mark Twain's *Huckleberry Finn* as both a point of reference and, as is the case with *Invisible Man*, a text to react against.

The narrator's journey in *Invisible Man* is more than a quest for selfhood. The novel's setting within the racially segregated United States allows Ellison to probe the way white supremacy distorts Americans' perceptions of themselves.

The narrator of *Invisible Man* seeks individual liberation through freedom from social oppression, but he finds this freedom only in solitude.

The Battle Royal scenes in *Invisible Man* feature sexual taboo as a means to condition the narrator for connection to larger systems of power and control. The Battle Royal itself is symbolic of the generation of black labor and its conversion into forms useful to white-controlled systems of capital.

Chapter 3: Contemporary Perspectives on Race

Introduction

Ralph Ellison's novel *Invisible Man* was widely lauded upon its publication in 1952, and the following year it won the National Book Award. Later, in 1965, a *Book Week* poll dubbed Ellison's novel the "most distinguished single work" published since World War II. Literary scholar Thomas Heise describes *Invisible Man* as a "story of maturation, a bildungsroman of a young black man whose life, Ellison says in his essays, is caught in the 'fluid, pluralistic turbulence' of America" ("Race, Writing, and Morality: Cultural Conversations in the Works of Ralph Ellison"). Heise adds that the novel is "about confronting change. And it is a book about how one endures in the face of seemingly insurmountable obstacles," a task that, he notes, Ellison believed in as an African American writer. In an interview in his 1964 collection of essays, *Shadow and Act*, Ellison claims that the role of the African American writer in particular "is that of preserving in art those human values which can endure by confronting change," even in the face of "the obstacles and meannesses imposed upon us."

As suggested by Ellison's views of himself as a writer, *Invisible Man* is not only about confronting personal change but also about enduring the sociopolitical changes of our day. In this light, *Invisible Man* is a "profoundly historical novel, invested and interested with history as a chronological idea and as a force shaping the present," literature scholar Andrew Allport writes in his essay "Literary Contexts in Novels: Ralph Ellison's *Invisible Man*." The historical force that shapes the life of Ellison's protagonist in the novel is the social milieu in the United States in the aftermath of World War II. As Allport and many other Ellison scholars note, the postwar years ushered in great changes for Americans and changed the lives of African Americans in particular.

After the war, the American economy thrived, and economic opportunities for African Americans increased with the new demand for industrial workers. Wages increased, and most workers' standards of living improved. The need for industrial workers in large cities such as Chicago, New York, and St. Louis spurred the movement of blacks from their agricultural jobs in the South to the new opportunities in the North. This geographical redistribution of African Americans had been occurring since the Great Migration of the 1910s and 1920s. In addition to the availability of jobs in the North, African American workers also encountered a greater sense of freedom. In the northern cities they were not subjected to segregation or the threat of lynch mobs that still terrorized the rural South. In *Invisible Man*, the protagonist's life in the North is plagued with its own brand of racial challenges, yet along with expanded social freedoms he also discovers more platforms through which his political voice can be heard.

Ellison's protagonist, the invisible man, does more than just document radical social and political changes. In Heise's words, the narrator "transforms the simmering tensions and flares of violence between blacks and whites into the black and white of the printed pages the reader holds in his hands." Readers reflect on these tensions long after they have closed the novel, however, as suggested by the ongoing critical response to the work.

The viewpoints that follow in this volume of *Social Issues in Literature* present a sampling of this critical response, providing further insight into the sociopolitical plight of African Americans through Ellison's handling of race in *Invisible Man*. Chapter 1, "Background on Ralph Ellison," places the novel in biographical and historical context. The viewpoints give a brief account of Ellison's life and his eagerness to become an American author. They examine Ellison's literary influences and his ultimate place in American literary history.

Chapter 2, "Race in *Invisible Man*," offers a range of literary criticism on characters, setting, themes, motifs, and other elements within the novel, relating specifically to issues of race. Some viewpoint authors discuss the racial and social significance of the work and place the text within the framework of the African American radicalism of Ellison's youth. Others examine the ways in which Ellison's protagonist strives to obtain racial equality and justice or democratic individuality. Additional critics analyze topics such as the racially charged symbols found throughout the novel and the social taboos that Ellison unmasks.

While the sociopolitical changes facing American culture in the early twenty-first century may not be as dramatic as those that occurred after World War II, the nation remains in a state of flux. Barack Obama, the first African American president of the United States, took office in January 2009, and according to Mark Dolliver in his essay "How Close Is Post-racial America?," in a 2009 opinion poll conducted by ABC News and the *Washington Post*, 64 to 70 percent of African Americans believed that "Obama's election 'represents progress for all blacks in America more in general' rather than just the triumph of one man." Scholars disagree, however, on just how much progress African Americans and other American minority groups have made. Chapter 3, "Contemporary Perspectives on Race," provides current viewpoints on race and its significance in American culture today.

Chronology

1914
Ralph Waldo Ellison is born in Oklahoma City, Oklahoma, on March 1 to Lewis Alfred Ellison and Ida Millsap Ellison.

1917
Ellison's father dies.

1920
Ellison enters the Frederick Douglass School in Oklahoma City.

1931
Ellison graduates from Douglass High School in Oklahoma City.

1933
Ellison attends Tuskegee Institute in Alabama as a scholarship student in music.

1936
Ellison leaves Tuskegee and heads to New York City to study sculpture. He meets the African American authors Langston Hughes and Richard Wright.

1937
Ellison's mother dies in February, in Dayton, Ohio. He publishes a book review in *New Challenge*, a magazine edited by Richard Wright.

1938–1942
Ellison is hired by the Federal Writers' Project to conduct oral-history research. He writes book reviews for *New Challenge*, *Direction*, *Negro Quarterly*, and *New Masses*. Ellison publishes several of his short stories, including "Slick Gonna Learn," "The Birthmark," "Afternoon," and "Mister Toussan."

1942

Ellison resigns from the Federal Writers' Project. He works as managing editor of the *Negro Quarterly*.

1943–1945

Ellison joins the Merchant Marine.

1945

Ellison is awarded a Rosenwald Foundation Fellowship to write a novel. He begins writing *Invisible Man*.

1946

Ellison marries Fanny McConnell.

1952

Ellison publishes *Invisible Man*, for which he receives the National Book Award and the Russwurm Award from the National Newspaper Publishers Association.

1955–1957

Ellison lives in Rome as a guest of the American Academy of Arts and Letters.

1958–1961

Ellison teaches Russian and American literature at Bard College in New York.

1960

Ellison publishes "Hickman Arrives," the first in a series of Hickman stories, in the London-based literary magazine *Noble Savage*.

1962–1964

Ellison teaches creative writing at Rutgers University.

1964

Shadow Act, containing essays, reviews, and interviews from 1942 to 1964, is published by Random House. Ellison becomes a fellow in American Studies at Yale.

1968

A fire in Ellison's summer house in Massachusetts destroys the manuscript of his second novel.

1969

Ellison is awarded the Medal of Freedom, America's highest civilian honor, by President Lyndon Johnson.

1970

Ellison is awarded the Chevalier de l'Ordre des Artes et Lettres by André Malraux, the French minister of cultural affairs.

1970–1980

Ellison is Albert Schweitzer Professor of Humanities at New York University.

1975

Ellison is elected to the American Academy of Arts and Letters. He speaks at the dedication of the Ralph Ellison Public Library in Oklahoma City.

1981

Ralph Ellison's Long Tongue, a mixed-media theater piece, is staged in New York.

1982

The thirtieth-anniversary edition of *Invisible Man* is published by Random House.

1984

Ellison is awarded the Langston Hughes Medal by City College of New York for his contributions to arts and letters.

1986

Ellison publishes *Going to the Territory*, a collection containing essays from 1957 to 1980.

1994

Ellison dies in Harlem on April 16 at age eighty. He is buried in Washington Heights in New York City.

1999

Ellison's second novel, *Juneteenth*, edited by Ellison's friend and literary executor, John F. Callahon, is published posthumously by Random House. The novel consists of 368 pages condensed from Ellison's 2,000-page manuscript.

2010

Expanded to 1,136 pages of the original manuscript, Ellison's second novel is rereleased as *Three Days Before the Shooting* by Modern Library.

Background on
Ralph Ellison

Ralph Ellison: The Man and His Work

Contemporary Literary Criticism

Ralph Waldo Ellison is one of America's most significant writers of the twentieth century. As noted in this viewpoint from Contemporary Literary Criticism, *Ellison is best known for his novel* Invisible Man. *In addition to including brief biographical information on Ellison, the editors offer a quick overview of the novel. They see Ellison's unnamed protagonist as ultimately understanding that he must accept social responsibility and live in the world, not outside of it. The editors also explore Ellison's influence as a critically acclaimed essayist and critic and touch on the plot and themes of Ellison's second novel, published posthumously as* Juneteenth. *Ellison maintained that* Invisible Man *is about an American man trying to define his values and forge an identity for himself. As the editors note, some critics complained that the novel strictly concerns black culture. Others, however, argue that it transcends racial boundaries and offers insight into universal experiences.*

Ralph Waldo Ellison was one of the most influential and accomplished American authors of the twentieth century. He was best known for his highly acclaimed novel *Invisible Man* (1952), a work that affirms the need for the individual to attain self-awareness. Honored with the National Book Award for fiction, *Invisible Man* is regarded as a masterpiece for its complex treatment of racial repression and betrayal. Shifting between naturalism, expressionism, and surrealism, Ellison combined concerns of European and African-American literature to chronicle an unnamed black youth's quest to discover his identity within a deluding, hostile world. Although critics have faulted Ellison's style as occasionally excessive, *Invisible Man* has consistently been praised for its poetic, ambiguous form, sustained blend of tragedy and comedy, and complex symbolism and characterizations.

Born in Oklahoma City, Oklahoma, on March 1, 1914, Ellison was raised in a cultural atmosphere that encouraged self-fulfillment. After studying music from 1933 to 1936 at Tuskegee Institute, a college founded by [educator and writer] Booker T. Washington to promote black scholarship, Ellison traveled to New York City, where he met author Richard Wright and became involved in the Federal Writers' Project. Encouraged to write a book review for *New Challenge*, a publication edited by Wright, Ellison began composing essays and stories that focus on the strength of the human spirit and the necessity for racial pride. Ellison died of cancer on April 16, 1994.

Major Works

Two of his most celebrated early short stories, "Flying Home" and "King of the Bingo Game," foreshadow Ellison's masterwork, *Invisible Man* (1952), in their portrayal of alienated young protagonists who seek social recognition. "Flying Home" is set during World War II and depicts a young black pilot whose obsessive desire to rid himself of stereotypes causes him to become contemptuous of his own race. After his airplane crashes, he is nursed back to health by a group of farmers who awaken his sense of cultural kinship and self-esteem. The anonymous protagonist of "King of the Bingo Game" is desperate to save his dying wife and enters a bingo tournament hoping to win enough money to hire a doctor. As the tournament proceeds, the bingo game becomes a symbol of his inability to control his destiny.

Although he originally envisioned writing a war novel, Ellison instead began work on *Invisible Man* following his honorable discharge from the United States Merchant Marines in

1945. His initial intention, to show the irony of black soldiers fighting for freedom who return to a civilian life of oppression, developed into a broader psychological study of the individual in society. Most critics consider the unspecified action of *Invisible Man* to take place between the early 1930s and 1950s. The novel's picaresque hero is often compared to [French Enlightenment writer] Voltaire's [protagonist in] *Candide*, who remains optimistic despite enduring betrayal, manipulation, humiliation, and the loss of his illusions. Narrating his story from an underground cell, the anonymous protagonist explains in the prologue that he is involuntarily invisible because society sees his social stereotype rather than his true personality. Establishing the novel's themes of betrayal and anonymity, the narrator recalls how he was raised in the South, named valedictorian of his high school graduation class, and invited to recite a speech for the community's prominent white citizens. This episode, which critics often refer to as Ellison's "battle royal" chapter, was originally published as a short story entitled "Invisible Man" in *Horizon* magazine. Among other degradations, the protagonist and several other black youths invited to the meeting are forced to participate in blind boxing matches and to crawl for money on an electrified carpet. Only after he has suffered these humiliations is the narrator allowed to recite his speech. Although largely ignored by the drunken gathering, Ellison's hero is presented with a college scholarship and assumes that education will help overcome the racial problems he encounters. The evening's brutality convinces him that he will be rewarded if he does what white people expect, and this naive assumption provokes an identity crisis.

While attending a Southern college that strongly resembles Tuskegee Institute, the protagonist is assigned to chauffeur Mr. Norton, a white philanthropist, and innocently takes him to visit Jim Trueblood, a disreputable sharecropper whom Norton believes to be a colorful storyteller in the folk tradition of

Uncle Remus. Upon hearing Trueblood's account of incest with his daughter, Norton is both horrified and fascinated by the indulgence in moral taboos that he himself has secretly considered transgressing. Many critics claim that this episode contains some of Ellison's finest dialogue and characterizations. By evoking society's reactions to Trueblood, Ellison refuted stereotypes of ethical, principled whites and decadent, unscrupulous blacks. Following Trueblood's revelation, the narrator takes Norton to a saloon called the Golden Day. The saloon's name refers to the Era of Reform between 1830 and 1860, during which many citizens entertained idealistic hopes of social reform that were later thwarted by industrialism and materialistic values. Norton's visit occurs at a time when the saloon is crowded with American veterans of World War I who, after fighting overseas for the freedom of others, were institutionalized for refusing to conform to segregation laws. One patron, a brilliant brain surgeon, later gives the narrator advice for his future: "[The] world is possibility if only you'll discover it." The narrator contemplates the surgeon's comment as he travels north, a move reminiscent of the Great Migration of the 1920s, when displaced southerners journeyed to the industrialized northern United States to obtain employment.

Expelled from college for his misadventure with Mr. Norton, Ellison's protagonist travels to the Harlem district of New York City in search of a job. He possesses sealed letters of reference from Doctor Bledsoe, president of his former university, that are later revealed to contain character defamations. The narrator nonetheless obtains employment with Liberty Paints, a company that manufactures white paint to be used in the bleaching of national monuments. As the result of an accident for which he is held responsible, the protagonist is hospitalized and given a form of electroshock therapy intended to mimic the effects of a lobotomy. Although desensitized, he vividly recalls the folklore of his Southern boyhood and emerges with a new sense of racial pride, while the super-ficiality of his previous experience is erased. For the first time he is unashamed of his background and asserts his disdain for servile blacks by dumping a spittoon on a man whom he mis-takes for Doctor Bledsoe.

Following an impromptu speech that he delivers on a street after discovering that an elderly couple have been evicted from their home, the narrator of *Invisible Man* attracts the at-tention of the Brotherhood, an organization that critics gener-ally equate with American Communist associations of the 1930s. After briefly embracing the group's utopian ideals, he discovers that the Brotherhood merely feigns interest in civil rights while actually working to repress blacks and deny their individuality. The chaos that ensues in the black community following the frenzied exhortations of a fanatic nationalist de-velops into a hallucinatory treatment of the Harlem race riots of the 1940s and culminates in the protagonist's final rejection of false identities. [Novelist] Wright Morris asserted: "Ellison handles this surrealist evening with so much authority and macabre humor, observing the forces with such detachment, that the reader is justified in feeling that in the process of mastering his rage, he has also mastered his art." Upon escap-ing the uproar of the riots, the narrator accidentally falls into a coal cellar that leads to the cell where he eventually achieves self-definition. Although he succumbs to anger by stealing electricity from the local power company, he deduces that his experiences have made him a unique individual. Despite his invisibility, the protagonist realizes that he must accept social responsibility and face the world.

Essayist and Critic

Ellison was also highly regarded for his accomplishments as an essayist. *Shadow and Act* (1964) collects twenty-two years of reviews, criticism, and interviews concerning such subjects as art, music, literature, and the influence of the black experi-

Portrait of Ralph Ellison, author of Invisible Man, *in 1964.* © Bettmann/Corbis.

ence on American culture. This acclaimed volume is often considered autobiographical in intent and is noted for its lucidity and insights into *Invisible Man. Going to the Territory*

(1986), which contains speeches, reviews, and interviews written since 1957, echoes many of the concerns of *Shadow and Act*. Making use of ironic humor in the manner of *Invisible Man*, Ellison here reflected on personal influences and paid tribute to such creative mentors as Richard Wright and [jazz pianist and bandleader] Duke Ellington. Ellison's short stories remain uncollected but are anthologized in such volumes as *A New Southern Harvest* (1957), *The Angry Black* (1962), and *Soon, One Morning: New Writing by American Negroes, 1940– 1962* (1963; published in Great Britain as *Black Voices*). The latter book contains "Out of the Hospital and under the Bar," a noted excerpt deleted from *Invisible Man*.

Ellison's influence as both novelist and critic, as artist and cultural historian, was enormous. A measure of his stature and achievement was his readers' vigil for his long-awaited second novel, left unfinished at his death. Although Ellison often refused to answer questions about the work-in-progress, there was evidence to suggest that the manuscript was very large, that all or part of it was destroyed in a fire and was being rewritten, and that its creation was a long and painful task. Most readers waited expectantly, believing that Ellison, who said in *Shadow and Act* that he "failed of eloquence" in *Invisible Man*, would not publish his second novel until it equaled his imaginative vision of the American novel as conqueror of the frontier and answered the Emersonian call for a literature to release all people from the bonds of oppression.

The Second Novel

Eight excerpts from this novel-in-progress have been published in literary journals. Set in the South in the years spanning the Jazz Age to the Civil Rights movement, these fragments seem an attempt to recreate modern American history and identity. The major characters are the Reverend Hickman, a one-time jazz musician, and Bliss, the light-skinned boy whom he adopts and who later passes into white society and becomes Senator Sunraider, an advocate of white supremacy. As Robert G. O'Meally noted in his 1980 study *The Craft of Ralph Ellison*, the major difference between Bliss and Ellison's earlier young protagonists is that despite some harsh collisions with reality, Bliss refuses to divest himself of his illusions and accept his personal history. Says O'Meally: "Moreover, it is a renunciation of the blackness of American experience and culture, a refusal to accept the American past in all its complexity."

Like *Invisible Man*, this novel promised to be a broad and searching inquiry into identity, ideologies, culture, and history. The narrative form is similar as well; here, too, is the blending of popular and classical myth, of contradictory cultural memories, of an intricate pattern of images of birth, death, and rebirth. In *Shadow and Act* Ellison described the novel's form as "a realism extended beyond realism." What the ultimate form of the novel would be—if, indeed, these excerpts were to be part of one novel—remained hidden. But the pieces seize the reader's imagination even if they deny systematic analysis.

One thing does seem certain about these stories. In them Bliss becomes a traitor to his own race, loses his hold on those things of transforming, affirmative value. Hickman, on the other hand, accepts and celebrates his heritage, his belief in the timeless value of his history. The tone of these excerpts is primarily tragicomic, a mode well-suited to Ellison's definition of life. As he wrote in *Shadow and Act*, "I think that the mixture of the marvelous and the terrible is a basic condition of human life and that the persistence of human ideals represents the marvelous pulling itself up out of the chaos of the universe." Elsewhere in the book, Ellison argued that "true novels, even when most pessimistic and bitter, arise out of an impulse to celebrate human life." As *Invisible Man* before, they celebrate the "human and absurd" commixture of American life.

Critical Reception

Although attacked by black nationalists for lacking stringent militancy toward civil rights issues, *Invisible Man* garnered laudatory reviews immediately following its publication and has continued to generate scholarly exegeses [interpretations]. Many critics have commented on how the book's dexterous style, dense symbolism, and narrative structure lend intricacy to its plot. The narrator, who reflects on his past experiences, is observed as both an idealistic, gullible youth and as an enlightened, responsible man who actively addresses problems that may result from social inequality. [Critic] Timothy Brennan declared: "[The] language and methods of the protest tradition are wielded by Ellison with an ambiguous voice, never finally pronouncing or judging, but building to a culmination of alternating hope and bitterness, rebellion and despair."

The most controversial issue concerning *Invisible Man* involves its classification as either a work written for and about Blacks alone or as a novel with universal import. Critics who insist the book strictly concerns black culture maintain that the experiences, emotions, and lifestyles described could not possibly be simulated by white authors, while supporters of the more prevalent view that *Invisible Man* transcends racial concerns contend that the protagonist's problems of illusion, betrayal, and self-awareness are experienced by every segment of society. Ellison himself asserted that *Invisible Man* is a novel that attempts to provide a portrait of the American individual who must define his values and himself despite a transitory existence. [Novelist] Jonathan Baumbach observed: "Refracted by satire, at times cartooned, Ellison's world is at once surreal and real, comic and tragic, grotesque and normal—our world viewed in its essentials rather than its externals. Though the protagonist of *Invisible Man* is a southern Negro, he is, in Ellison's rendering, profoundly all of us."

Ralph Ellison's Life and Literary Influences Helped Shape *Invisible Man*

Norman Podhoretz

Norman Podhoretz is editor at large of Commentary, *a conservative magazine about American intellectual life.*

In the following viewpoint, Podhoretz recalls Ralph Ellison's rise to instant fame after the publication of Invisible Man. *He describes the ways in which Ellison's first novel was unique in both substance and technique, and he examines Ellison's views about his cultural heritage and his place in American culture as a black writer. Podhoretz highlights Ellison's use of African folklore in his work, but he notes that Ellison credits his success as an author to both black and white literary influences. Ellison read a wide variety of literary classics to teach himself to become a writer, and as a coming-of-age story,* Invisible Man *is similar to some of the best American novels. Despite this similarity, Podhoretz argues,* Invisible Man *is not derivative of the authors Ellison admired.*

What [British prime minister] Winston Churchill said of the Battle of Britain—"Never ... was so much owed by so many to so few"—might with appropriate adaptations easily be applied to the American novelist Ralph Ellison. For surely no author ever owed so much to a single book: so much acclaim, so much honor, so many awards.

The novel in question, of course, is *Invisible Man*, which came out in 1952 when Ellison was already thirty-eight years old. Except for a few excerpts that had appeared while the

Norman Podhoretz, "What Happened to Ralph Ellison," *Commentary*, v. 108, no. 1, July 1999, p. 46. Copyright ©1999 by Commentary, Inc. All rights reserved. Reproduced by permission of the publisher.

book was still a work-in-progress, he had previously published only a number of reviews and a few stories of no particular distinction. But this first novel by an obscure Negro writer (to use the term in common currency in those far-off days) was immediately hailed on all sides as a classic, an imperishable masterpiece, perhaps the greatest American novel of the century. Accordingly, Ellison was elevated overnight into the upper reaches of our culture, and for the remaining 42 years of his life—he died in 1994 at the age of eighty—was treated reverently on the strength of this one book. . . .

On . . . Ellison's [side of the] street, it was usually sunny, and hardly any rain ever fell on his parade. Much more typical than the attacks of [critics] was the response of Ellison's fellow novelist, Saul Bellow: "What a great thing it is when a brilliant individual victory occurs, like Ellison's, proving that a truly heroic quality can exist among our contemporaries." It was mainly praise of this high order, and even higher, that came his way, and the few times he was criticized—by me, among others—it was for certain ideas expressed in his essays not for any faults or deficiencies that might have been unearthed in *Invisible Man* on a second or third reading, let alone a first.

New in Both Substance and Technique

The literary climate has changed very radically since 1952, to the point where many people have come to suspect the operation of a double standard whenever a black author wins the National Book Award or the Pulitzer or some other literary prize. It therefore seems necessary to state bluntly that the admiration Ellison evoked with *Invisible Man* emitted not the slightest whiff of critical affirmative action, and would not have done so even if such a concept had existed then (which mercifully it did not).

This is not to imply that Ellison's race went unnoticed. How could it? The word "novel" means new, and there was a time when the novelist saw it as his job either to bring the news of a world previously unexplored or to find a new way of performing that task on ground that may already have been broken and tilled and ploughed by others before him. In both of these senses—the substantive as well as the technical—Ellison was unmistakably and unabashedly, and proudly, a Negro novelist. As he himself defiantly declared: "Who wills to be a Negro? I do!"

Moreover, the "invisibility" he was making visible referred not only to the identity of his nameless hero. Even more broadly and crucially, it consisted of his effort to show that Negroes were very far from being an undifferentiated mass of suffering victims with no autonomous existence of their own—that they were not, in other words, a people wholly created and determined by forces controlled by the white world. This was how they had been, and still were (and to this day still are), most often portrayed by their own spokesmen, literary as well as political, black as well as white. But as Ellison never grew weary of saying in his essays and interviews, and as *Invisible Man* was written to "prove" in the way that only art can do, Negroes (even under slavery, let alone lesser forms of oppression) were fully human. . . .

Cultural Heritage Makes One an American

In speaking of the culture of the American Negro, Ellison did so first in the anthropological sense:

> Being a Negro American . . . has to do with a special perspective on the national ideals and the national conduct, and with a tragicomic attitude toward the universe. It has to do with special emotions evoked by the details of cities and countrysides, with forms of labor and with forms of pleasure; with sex and with love, with food and with drink, with machines and with animals, with garments and dreams and idioms of speech; with manners and customs, with religion and art, with lifestyles and hoping, and with that special

sense of predicament and fate which gives direction and resonance to the Freedom Movement.

Clearly with [author] Henry James's famous observation that it was a "complex fate" to be an American echoing in his head, Ellison went on to apply a version of the same concept to being an American Negro:

> It imposes the uneasy burden and occasional joy of a complex double vision, a fluid, ambivalent response to men and events which represents, at its finest, a profoundly civilized adjustment to the cost of being human in this modern world.

But when Ellison discussed culture, he naturally also had in mind the arts—especially the blues, jazz, and (on its own less self-conscious level) folklore—that had developed to give the deepest expression to the American Negro's special modes of thinking and speaking and being. Such expression was what he had aspired to achieve in *Invisible Man*, and it remained his ambition throughout his whole life.

However, distinctive as the Negro American culture may have been, Ellison—blasting an unbridgeable gulf between himself and the black nationalists whose rhetoric his own could sometimes misleadingly resemble when the celebratory spirit was upon him—also never tired of repeating that this culture was simultaneously American to the core:

> It is not skin color which makes a Negro American but cultural heritage as shaped by the American experience, the social and political predicament; a sharing of that "concord of sensibilities" which the group expresses through historical circumstances and through which it has come to constitute a subdivision of the larger American culture.

To Ellison this was a self-evident truth, although it too was "invisible" to most white people, and many blacks as well.

But most "invisible" of all was the correlatively pervasive interpenetration of the Negro culture and "the larger American culture," as well as the degree to which they drew from the same sources and had influenced and shaped each other. This is why he loved juxtaposing [musician] Louis Armstrong with the St. Louis born-and-bred [poet] T.S. Eliot, both of them children of the Mississippi River. Going even further, he always claimed that while he found Eliot's poem "The Waste Land" hard to understand when he first came upon it (in, as he often made a point of stressing polemically against those liberals who imagined that no such thing was possible, the library of Tuskegee, the black college he attended in the South), he could still detect in its obscure verses a resemblance to the offbeat jazzy rhythms that marked Armstrong's music....

Ellison's Literary Destiny

One might even say without too much exaggeration that Ellison had written *Invisible Man* precisely to give novelistic life and flesh to this previously most "invisible" of all the truths he was bent on bringing to light ("Who knows," runs the book's last sentence, "but that on the lower frequencies I speak for you?").

But there was another side to the same coin that has to be displayed if the picture is to be complete—and all the more so at a moment when thinking on these matters, while bearing a superficial similarity to Ellison's, is at the furthest remove from his. If most American whites were, in Ellison's unshakable view, "part Negro American without even realizing it," most Negroes were conversely more American than they or their white countrymen generally understood. There is a saying in Hebrew: "As his name is, so is he," and Ralph Waldo Ellison was a very good example of this peculiar phenomenon. That he had been named after one of the quintessentially American writers and sages [philosopher and writer Ralph Waldo Emerson] was something to which he and others often alluded as an amusing and even slightly embarrassing fact. But my own guess is that, deep down, he took it with great seriousness as a mark not only of his Americanness but of his literary destiny and his human fate.

Ellison had originally set out to pursue a career in music, and though he then had and would maintain a lifelong love affair with, and the profoundest admiration for, the music of the black world—most notably the blues and jazz—his ambition was (characteristically) to become a composer of classical symphonies. Then, when already into his twenties, he met [author] Richard Wright, who with the publication of *Native Son* (1940) was soon to emerge as the leading black novelist of the generation before Ellison's and who encouraged him to try his hand at writing. That did it. The young man's growing suspicion that he was not talented enough to realize his musical ambitions gave way to a more promising and positive intuition: that what he was truly cut out for was a literary career—though in talking about Ellison, a better term would be "vocation."

Yet it is of the utmost importance to emphasize again that Ellison's ambition was to become an American writer. As what used to be labeled a "pluralist," he believed in the existence of a common culture, one which the various ethnic and racial groups making up a heterogeneous society like ours steadily enriched by their indigenous contributions. This common culture was a precious heritage that could be claimed by any American of whatever group or color, and to it every American of whatever group or color also owed a debt and an allegiance. . . .

For Ellison, this balkanizing tendency was an ironic reappearance in sheep's clothing of the racial segregation under which he himself had grown up, and even may have been worse. Neither as a Negro kid in Oklahoma nor as a college student in Alabama was he prevented from reading books that opened his eyes and his mind and his imagination to a wider world of possibility; on the contrary, he was urged on, not discouraged, by teachers and other adults to do so. Later, even as a literary novice, he never felt himself to be "limited" in any respect by his race or defined by it as a writer. Hence it was not to other black novelists—not even his first sponsor Richard Wright—that he looked for models to be emulated. Still less did he think that it was their books he should study in trying to learn the new craft—"a very stern discipline," he called it—that he was so fiercely determined to master.

Both Black and White Literary Influences

One knows all this from the snippets of autobiography that frequently turn up in Ellison's essays and interviews, and from the resentment always aroused in him by any suggestion that he had been exclusively or even largely influenced by other black writers. For instance, he excoriated his old friend and "sparring partner," the critic Stanley Edgar Hyman, for assuming that the use of folklore in *Invisible Man* was a product of Ellison's race:

> I use folklore in my work not because I am a Negro, but because writers like [T.S.] Eliot and [James] Joyce made me conscious of the literary value of my folk inheritance. My cultural background, like that of most Americans, is dual (my middle name, sadly enough, is Waldo). . . . My point is that the Negro American writer is also an heir of the human experience which is literature, and this might well be more important to him than his living folk tradition.

On numerous other occasions, he also went out of his way to deny that this or that detail of *Invisible Man* had been inspired by Wright or some other black predecessor. A much more powerful literary influence on him when starting out as a writer, he often insisted, had been exerted by a French novelist, André Malraux (and—further to underscore his constant emphasis on the admixture of cultures—he would add that it had been the Negro poet Langston Hughes who had given him two of Malraux's novels to read).

In addition, it had been through three 19th-century novels, Emily Brontë's *Wuthering Heights*, Thomas Hardy's *Jude the Obscure*, and Feodor Dostoevsky's *Crime and Punishment*, that the artistic power of fiction had first made an impact on him as an undergraduate at Tuskegee. The American writers he most often cited in his pieces about literature were also all white: Mark Twain, Stephen Crane, Henry James, and Ernest Hemingway. And then—above all, as it would turn out—there was William Faulkner, a Southerner who, though still to some extent infected by racism, had in Ellison's judgment produced more truthful portraits of Negroes than any black or white-liberal Northern novelists had ever succeeded in doing. . . .

Ellison Was an Original Thinker

Invisible Man, written in the first person, is a kind of bildungsroman [coming-of-age novel] about an idealistic young Negro (Ellison never gives him a name) who begins as a student at a black college in the South dutifully hoping to become what once upon a time was known as a "credit to his race." But a naive error leads to his expulsion, and he then makes his way to Harlem. There, instead of eventually finding and forging an identity by which he can be recognized by others, he is subjected to a series of adventures (including a stint in the Communist party, disguised by Ellison for no very good reason as "the Brotherhood") which finally leave him with the realization that he is in fact faceless—that is, invisible—to everyone around him, whether black or white. They all want to make some use of him for whatever ends they happen to be pursuing, but nobody has the slightest desire to see or know him as the individual human being he is. Nor are they any more interested in confronting the realities of the world around them, to which they are as blind as they are to him.

So disillusioned does he become through this realization that he winds up living all by himself in an abandoned cellar. But in the closing pages he decides to end his hibernation and reemerge, as invisible as ever but capable now of telling his imaginary interlocutor "what was really happening when your eyes were looking through."

The *Invisible Man's* story unfolds in the manner of a classic picaresque novel, as one vivid character after another bursts with such incandescent clarity onto the scene that the reader's eyes are simply prevented from "looking through." These characters are collectively meant to penetrate the stereotypes that have hidden the great diversity of Negro life in America. They thus cover a very broad range: from the apparently meek but cunningly manipulative and malevolent black college president Dr. Bledsoe, with his bewilderingly complicated sense of the only way a Negro can successfully maneuver his way around a hostile white world; to the wildly colorful and semi-comic, semi-sinister black-nationalist demagogue of West Indian origin, Ras the Exhorter; to the handsome and troubled Communist militant Tod Clifton; to the brilliant con man and hustler Rinehart; to the lovingly warm-hearted Harlem landlady Miss Mary Rambo.

Swelling this huge cast are many other figures, both major and minor, among them a number of whites like Mr. Norton, the wealthy trustee of the protagonist's college, and the Communist leader Brother Jack, who are portrayed with the same clarity: a clarity that can be arrived at only by the nonapologetic "cold eye" of a true novelist working with all his might to achieve precisely that and nothing else (though the paradox is that he accomplishes much else along the way that escapes writers who go whoring after what, from the perspective of an artist, are always strange gods).

All this was astonishing enough. But what seemed equally amazing for a first novel—and what today, knowing as we now do how great a reader Ellison was and how diligently in learning to write fiction he schooled himself in other books, seems all the more amazing—was how underivative it was. If one looked closely enough, one could detect the influence here and there of this writer or that. But the main quality that struck so many of us on a first reading of *Invisible Man* was its originality: no such voice had ever been heard before in American literature.

A Conquest of the Frontier: An Interview with Ralph Ellison

Ralph Ellison, as told to Alfred Chester and Vilma Howard

Ralph Ellison was the author of Invisible Man. *Novelist Alfred Chester and poet and journalist Vilma Howard were both editors for the* Paris Review.

Chester and Howard interviewed Ralph Ellison about Invisible Man *in 1954. Ellison discusses the importance of African American folklore, describing it as a courageous expression that gave slaves a means to express their own experiences. He employs certain themes, symbols, and images in* Invisible Man *that are based on this black folk material. In writing* Invisible Man, *Ellison says, he intended to maintain consistent motivation for his protagonist in his search for identity in American culture. He also debunks the notion that his characters are based on real-life political or cultural figures. Finally, Ellison argues that African American experience touches a nerve in American consciousness. America's greatest authors, such as Mark Twain, Herman Melville, and William Faulkner, have explored a variety of themes emerging from this experience, and Ellison hopes his own novel will contribute to both the shaping and the growth of American literature and culture.*

In the summer of 1954, [Ralph] Ellison came abroad to travel and lecture. His visit ended in Paris where for a very few weeks he mingled with the American expatriate group to whom his work was known and of much interest. The day before he left he talked to [the *Paris Review*] in the Café de la Mairie du VIe about art and the novel. . . .

Alfred Chester and Vilma Howard, "Ralph Ellison, The Art of Fiction No. 8, Interview with Alfred Chester and Vilma Howard," *Paris Review*, Issue 8, Spring 1955. Copyright © 1955 by The Paris Review, Inc. Used with permission of The Wylie Agency LLC and the Estate of Alfred Chester.

Interviewer: How representative of the American nation would you say Negro folklore is?

Ellison: The history of the American Negro is a most intimate part of American history. Through the very process of slavery came the building of the United States. Negro folklore, evolving within a larger culture which regarded it as inferior, was an especially courageous expression. It announced the Negro's willingness to trust his own experience, his own sensibilities as to the definition of reality, rather than allow his masters to define these crucial matters for him. His experience is that of America and the West, and is as rich a body of experience as one would find anywhere. We can view it narrowly as something exotic, folksy, or "low-down," or we may identify ourselves with it and recognize it as an important segment of the larger American experience—not lying at the bottom of it, but intertwined, diffused in its very texture. I can't take this lightly or be impressed by those who cannot see its importance; it is important to *me*. One ironic witness to the beauty and the universality of this art is the fact that the descendants of the very men who enslaved us can now sing the spirituals and find in the singing an exaltation of their own humanity. Just take a look at some of the slave songs, blues, folk ballads; their possibilities for the writer are infinitely suggestive. Some of them have named human situations so well that a whole corps of writers could not exhaust their universality. For instance, here's an old slave verse:

Ole Aunt Dinah, she's just like me

She work so hard she want to be free

But ole Aunt Dinah's gittin' kinda ole

She's afraid to go to Canada on account of
the cold.

Ole Uncle Jack, now he's a mighty "good
nigger"

You tell him that you want to be free for a
fac'

Next thing you know they done stripped the
skin off your back.

Now ole Uncle Ned, he want to be free

He found his way north by the moss on the
tree

He cross that river floating in a tub

The patateroller [or patroller] give him a
mighty close rub.

It's crude, but in it you have three universal attitudes toward
the problem of freedom. You can refine it and sketch in the
psychological subtleties and historical and philosophical allusions, action and whatnot, but I don't think its basic definition can be exhausted. . . .

Invisible Man Contains Ritual Situations

*Can you give us an example of the use of folklore in your own
novel?*

Well, there are certain themes, symbols, and images which
are based on folk material. For example, there is the old saying among Negroes: If you're black, stay back; if you're brown,
stick around; if you're white, you're right. And there is the
joke Negroes tell on themselves about their being so black
they can't be seen in the dark. In my book this sort of thing
was merged with the meanings which blackness and light have
long had in Western mythology: evil and goodness, ignorance
and knowledge, and so on. In my novel the narrator's development is one through blackness to light; that is, from ignorance to enlightenment, invisibility to visibility. He leaves the
South and goes North; this, as you will notice in reading Negro folk tales, is always the road to freedom—the movement
upward. You have the same thing again when he leaves his underground cave for the open.

It took me a long time to learn how to adapt such examples of myth into my work—also ritual. The use of ritual is equally a vital part of the creative process. I learned a few things from [T.S.] Eliot, [James] Joyce and [Ernest] Hemingway, but not how to adapt them. When I started writing, I knew that in both "The Waste Land" and *Ulysses* [by Eliot and Joyce, respectively], ancient myth and ritual were used to give form and significance to the material; but it took me a few years to realize that the myths and rites which we find functioning in our everyday lives could be used in the same way. In my first attempt at a novel, which I was unable to complete, I began by trying to manipulate the simple structural unities of *beginning, middle, and end*, but when I attempted to deal with the psychological strata—the images, symbols, and emotional configurations—of the experience at hand, I discovered that the unities were simply cool points of stability on which one could suspend the narrative line, and that beneath the surface of apparently rational human relationships there seethed a chaos before which I was helpless. People rationalize what they shun or are incapable of dealing with; these superstitions and their rationalizations become ritual as they govern behavior. The rituals become social forms, and it is one of the functions of the artist to recognize them and raise them to the level of art.

I don't know whether I'm getting this over or not. Let's put it this way: Take the "Battle Royal" passage in my novel, where the boys are blindfolded and forced to fight each other for the amusement of the white observers. This is a vital part of behavior pattern in the South, which both Negroes and whites thoughtlessly accept. It is a ritual in preservation of caste lines, a keeping of taboo to appease the gods and ward off bad luck. It is also the initiation ritual to which all greenhorns [newcomers] are subjected. This passage states what Negroes will see I did not have to invent; the patterns were already there in society so that all I had to do was present them in a broader context of meaning. In any society there are many rituals of situation which, for the most part, go unquestioned. They can be simple or elaborate, but they are the connective tissue between the work of art and the audience.

Do you think a reader unacquainted with this folklore can properly understand your work?

Yes, I think so. It's like jazz; there's no inherent problem which prohibits understanding but the assumptions brought to it. We don't all dig [playwright William] Shakespeare uniformly, or even "Little Red Riding Hood." The understanding of art depends finally upon one's willingness to extend one's humanity and one's knowledge of human life. I noticed, incidentally, that the Germans, having no special caste assumptions concerning American Negroes, dealt with my work simply as a novel. I think the Americans will come to view it that way in twenty years—if it's around that long.

Don't you think it will be?

I doubt it. It's not an important novel. I failed of eloquence and many of the immediate issues are rapidly fading away. If it does last, it will be simply because there are things going on in its depth that are of more permanent interest than on its surface. I hope so, anyway. . . .

From Purpose to Passion to Perception

When did you begin Invisible Man?

In the summer of 1945. I had returned from the sea, ill, with advice to get some rest. Part of my illness was due, no doubt, to the fact that I had not been able to write a novel for which I'd received a Rosenwald Fellowship the previous winter. So on a farm in Vermont, where I was reading *The Hero* by Lord Raglan and speculating on the nature of Negro leadership in the U.S., I wrote the first paragraph of *Invisible Man*, and was soon involved in the struggle of creating the novel.

How long did it take you to write it?

Author Ralph Ellison testifies at a US Senate subcommittee hearing on racial conflict in urban areas, August 30, 1966. © AP Photo.

Five years with one year out for a short novel which was unsatisfactory, ill-conceived, and never submitted for publication.

Did you have everything thought out before you began to write Invisible Man?

The symbols and their connections were known to me. I began it with a chart of the three-part division. It was a conceptual frame with most of the ideas and some incidents indicated. The three parts represent the narrator's movement from, using [critic] Kenneth Burke's terms, purpose to passion to perception. These three major sections are built up of smaller units of three which mark the course of the action and which depend for their development upon what I hoped was a consistent and developing motivation. However, you'll note that the maximum insight on the hero's part isn't reached until the final section. After all, it's a novel about innocence and human error, a struggle through illusion to reality. Each section begins with a sheet of paper; each piece of paper is exchanged for another and contains a definition of his identity, or the social role he is to play as defined for him by others. But all say essentially the same thing: "Keep this nigger boy running." Before he could have some voice in his own destiny, he had to discard these old identities and illusions; his enlightenment couldn't come until then. Once he recognizes the hole of darkness into which these papers put him, he has to burn them. That's the plan and the intention; whether I achieved this is something else.

Would you say that the search for identity is primarily an American theme?

It is *the* American theme. The nature of our society is such that we are prevented from knowing who we are. It is still a young society, and this is an integral part of its development. . . .

The Author in Control of His Characters

Do you have any difficulty controlling your characters? [British novelist] E.M. Forster says that he sometimes finds a character running away with him.

No, because I find that a sense of the ritual understructure of the fiction helps to guide the creation of characters. Action is the thing. We are what we do and do not do. The problem for me is to get from A to B to C. My anxiety about transitions greatly prolonged the writing of my book. The naturalists stick to case histories and sociology and are willing to compete with the camera and the tape recorder. I despise concreteness in writing, but when reality is deranged in fiction, one must worry about the seams.

Do you have difficulty turning real characters into fiction?

Real characters are just a limitation. It's like turning your own life into fiction: you have to be hindered by chronology and fact. A number of the characters just jumped out, like Rinehart and Ras.

Isn't Ras based on Marcus Garvey [Jamaican-born black leader who established the first branch of his Universal Negro Improvement Association in the United States in 1917]?

No. In 1950 my wife and I were staying at a vacation spot where we met some white liberals who thought the best way to be friendly was to tell us what it was like to be Negro. I got mad at hearing this from people who otherwise seemed very intelligent. I had already sketched Ras, but the passion of his statement came out after I went upstairs that night feeling that we needed to have this thing out once and for all and get it done with; then we could go on living like people and individuals. No conscious reference to Garvey is intended.

What about Rinehart? Is he related to Rinehart in the blues tradition, or Django Reinhardt, the jazz musician?

There is a peculiar set of circumstances connected with my choice of that name. My old Oklahoma friend, Jimmy Rushing, the blues singer, used to sing one with a refrain that went:

Rinehart, Rinehart,

it's so lonesome up here

on Beacon Hill,

which haunted me, and as I was thinking of a character who was a master of disguise, of coincidence, this name with its suggestion of inner and outer came to my mind. Later I learned that it was a call used by Harvard students when they prepared to riot, a call to chaos. Which is very interesting, because it is not long after Rinehart appears in my novel that the riot breaks out in Harlem. Rinehart is my name for the personification of chaos. He is also intended to represent America and change. He has lived so long with chaos that he knows how to manipulate it. It is the old theme of [Herman Melville's] *The Confidence Man*. He is a figure in a country with no solid past or stable class lines; therefore he is able to move about easily from one to the other. . . .

The Novel Creates Experience

You know, I'm still thinking of your question about the use of Negro experience as material for fiction. One function of serious literature is to deal with the moral core of a given society. Well, in the United States the Negro and his status have always stood for that moral concern. He symbolizes among other things the human and social possibility of equality. This is the moral question raised in our two great nineteenth-century novels, *Moby-Dick* [by Herman Melville] and *Huckleberry Finn* [by Mark Twain]. The very center of Twain's book revolves finally around the boy's relations with Nigger Jim and the question of what Huck should do about getting Jim free after the two scoundrels had sold him. There is a magic here worth conjuring, and that reaches to the very nerve of the American consciousness—so why should I abandon it? Our so-called race problem has now lined up with the world problems of colonialism and the struggle of the West to gain the allegiance of the remaining non-white people who have thus far remained outside the communist sphere; thus its possibilities for art have increased rather than lessened. Looking at the novelist as manipulator and depicter of moral problems, I ask myself how much of the achievement of democratic ideals in the U.S. has been affected by the steady pressure of Negroes and those whites who were sensitive to the implications of our condition, and I know that without that pressure the position of our country before the world would be much more serious than it is even now. Here is part of the social dynamics of a great society. Perhaps the discomfort about protest in books by Negro authors comes because since the nineteenth century, American literature has avoided profound moral searching. It was too painful and besides there were specific problems of language and form to which the writers could address themselves. They did wonderful things, but perhaps they left the real problems untouched. There are exceptions, of course, like Faulkner who has been working the great moral theme all along, taking it up where Mark Twain put it down.

I feel that with my decision to devote myself to the novel I took on one of the responsibilities inherited by those who practice the craft in the U.S.: that of describing for all that fragment of the huge diverse American experience which I know best, and which offers me the possibility of contributing not only to the growth of the literature but to the shaping of the culture as I should like it to be. The American novel is in this sense a conquest of the frontier; as it describes our experience, it creates it.

Race in *Invisible Man*

Invisible Man Retains Its Racial and Social Relevance

Thomas R. Whitaker

Thomas R. Whitaker is a professor of English and theater studies at Yale University.

In this article, Whitaker maintains that despite changes in American politics and society, Invisible Man *retains its social relevance decades later. Ellison's narrator becomes disillusioned as he struggles to forge an identity in a racist society that renders him invisible. Nonetheless, Whitaker argues that as a spokesman, Ellison's narrator remains eloquent, gaining his authority to speak for others through his invisible relationship with his listeners. The narrator, however, remains invisible because of his skin color and the fact that he lives outside of what Whitaker calls organizational or official history. Ellison's protagonist fails to conform to others' definitions of him as a black man, but he, too, has been blinded by these definitions. It is not until the narrator emerges from underground in a ritual of rebirth that he is able to forgo the multiple identities others have constructed for him throughout the text and simply recall his earlier, true identity.*

"I am an invisible man." More than thirty years after the first publication of that famous opening sentence, some readers may find it hard to credit the notion that Americans who can claim African ancestry are in any sense "invisible." For quite a while [now, in 1987,] Tom Bradley has been mayor of Los Angeles, Andrew Young mayor of Atlanta, and Coleman Young mayor of Detroit. After the more recent election of Harold Washington as mayor of Chicago, there were 224 "black" mayors, 347 "black" state legislators, and twenty-one "black" congressmen in the United States. Citing those figures, *Newsweek* declared that "blacks" have now demonstrated their ability to reach beyond "their own community" and "reshape the politics of this nation."

Though our changing politics will make it harder to read Ralph Ellison's *Invisible Man* as a sign of the times, it doesn't follow that this realistic, comic, grotesque, allegorical, and nearly apocalyptic book is outdated. Its most obvious satirical targets are still with us: racial prejudice, blind and deceptive leadership, and the betrayal of America's promise. And its most obvious positive values remain necessary for the health of our body politic: a belief in the importance of the "forms of American Negro humanity," as Ellison called them in *Shadow and Act,* and a final precarious affirmation of "the principle on which the country was built."

That affirmation is necessary, Ellison's protagonist and narrator surmises, because "we, through no fault of our own, were linked to all the others in the loud, clamoring semi-visible world." He knows, as the staff of *Newsweek* apparently does not, that talk of "blacks" and "their own community" can refer to no ultimate or even unambiguous categories. He recounts in his Prologue a reefer-dream shaped by ambivalence in which a preacher expounded the "Blackness of Blackness" by shouting that *"black is"* and *"black ain't."* And he later tells us how "Optic White" is made at Liberty Paints by adding color to a base prepared underground by the Negro engineer, Lucius Brockway, and then mixing in some drops of "dead black" dope. The explosion in Brockway's engineroom sent him flying "into a wet blast of black emptiness that was somehow a bath of whiteness." Again and again he has found that "blackness" and "whiteness" are mutually defining and mutually inclusive—as ambiguous as the metaphysical "whiteness" that, a century earlier, troubled the Ishmael imagined by [novelist Herman] Melville, one of the "ancestors" to whom Ellison has paid tribute in "Hidden Name and Complex Fate."

Ellison's protagonist has also learned what Melville had implied [in *Moby Dick*] through the mixed crew of the *Pequod*, and another "ancestor" through the mixed crew of Huck Finn's raft [in a novel by Mark Twain]: "black" and "white" belong to the same community of ethical obligation and problematic identity. The "black" preacher Homer Barbee is as blind as the "white" sleepwalkers who don't recognize a "black" man's presence. The "white" Brother Jack, with his hypnotic glass eye, sees no more than did the "ginger colored" protagonist he was deceiving. The doomed youth leader, Tod Clifton, has "the chiseled, black-marble features sometimes found on statues in northern museums and alive in southern towns in which the white offspring of house children and the black offspring of yard children bear names, features and character traits as identical as the rifling of bullets fired from a common barrel." And the protagonist's gropings toward identity can proceed quite appropriately from his memory of a teacher's critique of [Irish author James] Joyce's *Portrait of the Artist as a Young Man* ("Stephen's problem, like ours; was not actually one of creating the uncreated conscience of his race, but of *creating the uncreated features of his face*") to his own reverie on the portrait of [American slave and author] Frederick Douglass: "What had his true name been? Whatever it was, it was as Douglass that he became himself, defined himself."

By the time he tells his story, of course, the protagonist has become disillusioned with the "faces" or "self-definitions" he had constructed in running either for or from "the Jacks and the Emersons and the Bledsoes and Nortons," and he has decided to run "only from their confusion, impatience, and refusal to recognize the beautiful absurdity of their American identity and mine." . . .

The Narrator's Eloquence

Must we decide, then, whether our spokesman is an absence, a metaphor for chaos, an antihero caught between death and resurrection, an agent of responsible freedom who has now defined himself, an emergent author in control of the imagination, an Emersonian [reminiscent of the works of philosopher and writer Ralph Waldo Emerson] transparent eyeball, or a black man whose identity is rooted in the vernacular tradition? Perhaps not. Such diverse readings suggest an indeterminacy or plurality of meaning in the book itself. The protagonist may be all of these things, and more besides, in ways that we have yet to explore. And we might start with Ellison's own remarks in 1955 to interviewers from the *Paris Review:* "It's not an important novel," he said. "I failed of eloquence, and many of the immediate issues are rapidly fading away. If it does last, it will be simply because there are things going on in its depth that are of more permanent interest than on its surface."

At first glance, that is a startling confession of failure. It seems to echo the narrator's own rueful remark about his final meeting with Ras the Exhorter: "But even as I spoke I knew it was no good. I had no words and no eloquence." For the narrator, "eloquence" often means the persuasive "magic in spoken words" that he recognizes with admiration or uneasiness in such various styles as Homer Barbee's incantatory sermon, Peter Wheatstraw's boasts and patter, and Ras's "crude, insane" pleas—the magic he can produce only when "another self" within him has "taken over and held forth." Eloquence for him arises from an invisible source and requires some tacit relation between speaker and hearers. Indeed, he has found that it doesn't need to be verbal. Describing his speeches downtown for the Brotherhood, he says: "I acted out a pantomime more eloquent than my most expressive words. I was a partner to it but could no more fathom it than I could the mystery of the man in the doorway." His comparison is apt: that image of a man in the doorway, which he had seen after a wealthy white woman had tempted him into her bed, may or may not have been a dream but certainly corresponded to his own fear and desire. And such hallucinatory eloquence of appearances has pervaded his life. He has moved in a psychic field that repeatedly manifests itself in speaking objects—Tod's dancing doll, Jack's glass eye, Tarp's chain link with "a heap of signifying wrapped up in it"—and in speakers without great talent who can express the pattern of an unconsciously shared situation. Even now he often seems unaware of the full meaning of such eloquence. When he relates Jim Trueblood's tale of incestuous dreamwork, he admits only that he had been "torn between humiliation and fascination." We can see, however, that Trueblood's tale symbolically mirrors not only Mr. Norton's repressed relation to his daughter and compensatory relation to the black college but also the protagonist's own Oedipal [named for the Greek tragedy of Oedipus] entrapment by that black-and-white structure of authority. And when he finally suggests that he himself may speak "for" us, we recognize a possibility that would gather up all the participatory eloquence of his world in an inclusive instance. . . .

Black and Invisible

"I was a *spokesman*," the protagonist had once insisted, "—why shouldn't I speak about women, or any other subject?" After he has burnt up his more hopeful "names" or "self-definitions"—the eager student, the willing worker, the charismatic orator—he retains that incompletely defined function. Invisible and without substance, he may speak for us. But what can this mean? His invisibility has more leaves than the onion to which [playwright Henrik] Ibsen's Peer Gynt had compared his own histrionic nonidentity.

He has been invisible, of course, because he is "black." When people of exclusively Caucasian ancestry look in his direction, they see only his surroundings, themselves, or figments of their imagination. But his invisibility has simply been exacerbated by his skin color. As a student at college, as an agent for President Bledsoe and a beneficiary of Mr. Norton, as a worker for Liberty Paints, and as a spokesman

A sculpture memorializing Invisible Man *is unveiled on May 1, 2003, in front of the west Harlem apartment complex where author Ralph Ellison lived for more than thirty years.* © AP Photo/Frank Franklin II.

for the Brotherhood, he has also been invisible. Anyone who enters structure of power tends not be seen by those who wield that power. Jack and Hambro, he learns, "didn't see either color or men.... I was simply a material, a natural resource to be used." Because we are all members of minority groups and because we are all used as means to the economic, political, and psychological ends through which others try to define themselves, the narrator speaks for us.

But he has also been invisible because, like Tod Clifton, he has fallen outside organizational or official history. Clifton had effectively foretold that fate in his wry comment on Ras ("I suppose sometimes a man *has* to plunge outside history"), and the protagonist poignantly apprehends it, at the Faulknerian [reminiscent of William Faulkner's works] moment of Clifton's death, through a fortuitous image of flight:

> I saw a flight of pigeons whirl out of the trees and it all happened in the swift interval of their circling . . . just as the cop pushed him, jolting him forward and Clifton trying to keep the box from swinging against his leg and saying something over his shoulder and going forward as one of the pigeons swung down into the street and up again, leaving a feather floating white in the dazzling backlight of the sun. . . .

That image haunts his later thoughts of Clifton:

> Where were the historians today? And how would they put it down? . . . What did they ever think of us transitory ones? Ones such as I had been before I found the Brotherhood— birds of passage who were too obscure for learned classification, too silent for the most sensitive recorders of sound; of natures too ambiguous for the most ambiguous words, and too distant from the centers of historical decision to sign or even to applaud the signers of historical documents?

Those boys seen in the subway, fresh from the South, speaking "a jived-up transitional language" and thinking "transitional thoughts, though perhaps they dream the same old ancient dreams," were such birds of passage. They were "men out of time"—but "who knew but that they were the saviors, the true leaders, the bearers of something precious?" . . .

But it's not just a matter of the blindness of official history. More fundamentally yet, the narrator has been invisible because he doesn't conform to the patterns of reality that others have defined for themselves. "Step outside the narrow borders of what men call reality," he says in the Epilogue, "and you step into chaos—ask Rinehart, he's a master of it—or imagination". Clinging to their certainties, refusing to exercise imagination, people blind themselves to the unique possibilities that seem to be "chaos." The protagonist knows, as [Ralph Waldo] Emerson and [Walt] Whitman did before him, that "Our fate is to become one, and yet many—This is not prophecy, but description." And because the reality of each of us is always at least partly invisible to those who have defined a different reality, he speaks for us.

The Responsibility for One's Invisibility

It follows, of course, that he has also been invisible because he too has been blind. At least "half" of his "sickness," he says, lay within him. Exploitation depends on our willingness to accept the "names" or "identities" foisted upon us. For a long time he couldn't see beyond the hope or glamour suggested by such names. Only when taken for "Rine the runner and Rine the gambler and Rine the briber and Rine the lover and Rinehart the Reverend" did he recognize that he moved in a society of role-playing to which the confidence-man had found one kind of solution. Frustrated now by the awareness that names designate masks, he was tempted to "do a Rinehart" and gain control of the whole charade. When that boomeranged in moral revulsion during his evening with Sybil—"Such games were for Rinehart, not me"—he had to admit that even an invisible power tempted by possibility must, if human, acknowledge a moral obligation to another human being. Then he ran in the night, and within himself, until his moment of truth in the midst of the Harlem riot. Facing Ras without "eloquence," he recognized the "beautiful absurdity" of the "American identity" compounded of "hope and desire, fear and hate," that had kept him running:

> I stood there, knowing that by dying, that by being hanged by Ras on this street in this destructive night I would perhaps move them one fraction of a bloody step closer to a definition of who they were and of what I was and had been. But the definition would have been too narrow; I was invisible. . . .

Because we blind ourselves to the inadequacy of the names given us by others, or exploit that inadequacy by blinding ourselves to the obligations that link us together in our invisible reality, he speaks for us.

After recognizing all this, he still remains invisible because he can't perform any action, however authentic, or formulate any self-definition, however accurate, that would disclose him as a determinate individual. . . . Knowing that "it was better to live out one's own absurdity than to die for that of others, whether for Ras's or Jack's," the protagonist let fly the spear at Ras—"and it was as though for a moment I had surrendered my life and begun to live again." Even what an existentialist might call an authentic action has only a momentary validity. Now, after being chased underground, he must endure the nightmare that expresses the emptiness of his freedom from illusion. . . .

A Ritual Rebirth

"The end was in the beginning," he tells us. And for him . . . that will always be so. He has made a "decision" to emerge from his hole, but he hasn't yet emerged. Though free to take the next step, he will even then be invisible. And that situation will recur in new forms, no matter what choices he makes. That's why he says: "I'm shaking off the old skin and I'll leave it here in the hole. I'm coming out, no less invisible without it, but coming out nevertheless." That old skin may be his story—or did you think he found a publisher? It is certainly the conflict-ridden "I" that his story has finally defined, an "I" still caught between yes and no, love and hate, denunciation and defense, the bad air and the good music it makes. If he emerges without that skin, we won't be able to see him. ". . . I've overstayed my hibernation," he says at last, "since there's a possibility that even an invisible man has a socially responsible role to play." There is no reason to believe that note to be faked. And because, though appearing to be distinct objects, we all participate in a free and answerable subjectivity, the protagonist speaks for us.

We have arrived at part of Ellison's answer to what [critic] Kenneth Burke, in *Attitudes Toward History*, had posited as the central literary problem, that of "identity." The naturalists, Burke said, had "discovered accurately enough that identity is *not* individual" but had resisted their own discovery. He argued that the "so-called 'I' is merely a unique combination of partially conflicting 'corporate we's.'" For everyone, a "change of identity" will occur "as any given structure of society calls forth conflicts among our 'corporate we's.' From this necessity you get, in art, the various ritualizations of rebirth." Such rituals "dredge" the problem of "How much of one's past identity must be forgotten, how much remolded, as he moves from one role to the next." It followed that "Change of identity is a way of 'seeing around the corner.'"

Ellison told interviewers from *Y'Bird Reader* in 1977 that Burke had "provided a *Gestalt* [backdrop] through which I could apply intellectual insights back into my own materials and into my own life." And in fact *Invisible Man* is a "ritual of rebirth" in which the protagonist, after several changes of identity, remembers his earlier life with an undeniably Burkean effect: "It was as though I'd suddenly learned to look around corners." But if he understands at last, as [critic Robert]

O'Meally has argued, that "he is, simply, who he is," he also knows that "isness" to be a manifold invisibility.

Invisible Man and African American Radicalism

Christopher Z. Hobson

Christopher Z. Hobson is associate professor of humanities and languages at the College at Old Westbury, State University of New York.

In this viewpoint, Hobson argues that Invisible Man *bears a relationship to the African American radicalism of Ellison's youth in the 1930s and early 1940s. The Brotherhood portrayed in the novel is allegorical of the Communist Party and its aggressive recruitment of African American members during this era. Work of the Brotherhood corresponds schematically to efforts of the Communist Party and likewise changes within the party with the start of World War II. Ellison depicts these changes as a sacrifice of the needs of black Brotherhood members in Harlem in favor of the party's new allegiances with other political groups. Hobson maintains that despite these shifting affinities within the Brotherhood, African American radicalism in* Invisible Man *not only affirms possibilities for social reform but also forecasts African Americans' struggles for civil rights in the decades subsequent to the publication of the novel.*

Ralph Ellison's *Invisible Man* bears a complex, ambiguous, and ultimately extraordinarily rich relation to the milieu that gave it birth, African American social radicalism in the late 1930s and early 1940s. Rather than simply providing background for a shift toward a more individualistic, artistic, or private life stance, *Invisible Man*'s relation to the radicalism of its author's youth is the source of its definition of an alternative basis for African American social struggle after the Broth-

Christopher Z. Hobson, "Invisible Man and African American Radicalism in World War II," *African American Review*, v. 39, 2005. Copyright © 2005 by Christopher Z. Hobson. All rights reserved. Reproduced by permission.

erhood experience, its continuing (if muted) affirmation of possibilities for social reform, and its forecast of the actual content of civil rights actions in the decades after its publication. Further, *Invisible Man*'s continuing relation to the African American radicalism of its time helps explain the oft-noted ambivalence of its conclusion on such matters as artistic and political action and individual as opposed to group freedom. These aspects of the novel reflect the overlapping contexts of African Americans' experiences in the Communist Party (hereafter CP) and, even more centrally, their responses to World War II, elements of history that are presented with specificity yet with mythic scope and resonance. . . .

The novel's Harlem sections, implicitly set during the 1930s and World War II, portray its protagonist's political education and transition between political philosophies. Here Ellison describes distinct phases in the work of his fictitious radical organization, the Brotherhood, that knowledgeable readers would associate with shifts in the work of the Communist Party during those years, and he incorporates other elements of plot, description, and atmosphere that reflect the evolution of many African American leftists away from the Communists and toward independent radicalism during the war. These aspects of *Invisible Man*, especially the latter, give the novel's second half its specific focus, tone, and overt socio-political content.

The Brotherhood as the Communist Party

Though the latter development is ultimately crucial for the protagonist's outlook, Ellison's portrayal of the Brotherhood provides its point of departure. The Harlem chapters sketch three periods in the organization's work. In the first (chaps. 13–16) the Brotherhood is pursuing an initial change in orientation, against semifactional resistance, from a more theoretical to a more popular style of agitation. Here, for example, we see Jack flatter the protagonist by contrast with Brotherhood speakers: "With a few words you have involved them in action! Others would have still been wasting time with empty verbiage." Jack and others speak of the need for new methods in "the coming period" and excoriate "sideline theoreticians." The heyday of the new orientation (chaps. 17–18) is a period of increased presence in Harlem, mass actions, popularization of the Brotherhood's message, and alliances with community leaders: the organization challenges Ras's nationalist grouping for influence in the streets, conducts a march to City Hall, and creates a multiracial "Rainbow" poster that, Brother Tarp testifies, Harlemites "[tack] to their walls 'long with 'God Bless Our Home' and the Lord's Prayer." Finally the leaders engineer a second reorientation (chaps. 20–23) in which they downgrade Harlem work in response to "a new program which had called for shelving our old techniques of agitation. There was, to [the protagonist's] surprise, a switch in emphasis from local issues to those more national and international in scope, and it was felt that for the moment, the interests of Harlem were not of first importance." As Brother Hambro elaborates, "We are making temporary alliances with other political groups and the interests of one group of brothers must be sacrificed to that of the whole."

These phases, of which the last will concern me most, correspond in a schematic way to similar episodes in the Communist party's work: the turn from "maximalist" revolutionary agitation (the so-called "Third Period" policy) to the "People's Front" or "Popular Front" in the mid-1930s; the height of the People's Front, a time of mass reform work, alliances with liberal forces, and aggressive recruitment of African Americans into the party; and the later deemphasis on militant agitation in response to the USSR's [Union of Soviet Socialist Republics'] entry into World War II (June 1941). Secondary details reinforce the novel's specific reference to the Communist Party. For example, Jack's comment that the Brotherhood is searching for new [Thomas] Jeffersons and [author and political leader] Booker T. Washingtons recalls the CP's effort during the "People's Front" to cast itself as perpetuator of US revolutionary traditions; Jack's later statement about Harlem community notables, "[W]e've always avoided these leaders, but the moment we start to advance on a broad front, sectarianism becomes a burden," evokes efforts to ally with "reformist" forces at the height of the "People's Front"; and the Brotherhood's later shift away from Harlem work has similarities in mood and consequence . . . with the CP's shifts just before and during the war. In keeping with his overall preferences in fiction, Ellison's portrayal is mythic and generalized; in particular, he omits anything corresponding to the period of the [Josef] Stalin–[Adolf] Hitler pact, when the world's Communist parties abandoned their earlier calls for unity against fascism, denounced the war as interimperialist, and strove to intensify struggle on class and democratic issues. Ellison lets the Brotherhood's "international" turn do the work for both historical episodes. Nonetheless, those familiar with shifts in Communist policies from the early 1930s up through the war years should recognize in the novel's pages a compressed, heightened, and allegorized version of those changes.

Though Ellison's treatment is ultimately critical, one cannot feel the depth and force of the criticism without understanding the power of the Brotherhood's attraction for the protagonist and thousands more. We can feel this appeal in the protagonist's words during his "dispossession" speech: "Something strange and miraculous and transforming is taking place in me right now . . . as I stand here before you! . . . I feel, I feel suddenly that I have become more human. . . . I feel I can see sharp and clear and far down the dim corridor of history and in it I can hear the footsteps of militant fraternity! . . . With your eyes upon me I feel that I've found my true family! My true people! My true country!" Here as elsewhere, Ellison echoes the Communist experiences of his friend [writer] Richard Wright, who wrote of his own entry into the party: "It was not the economics of Communism . . . that claimed me; my attention was caught . . . by the possibility of uniting scattered but kindred peoples into a whole. It seemed to me that here at last, in the realm of revolutionary expression, Negro experience could find a home." Like Wright, who describes feeling that the Communist Party could create "a new sense of reality . . . a sense of man on earth," Ellison's protagonist feels, despite his criticisms, that the Brotherhood provides "the only historically meaningful life." And the strength of these hopes is felt when the protagonist, unsure at Tod Clifton's funeral whether the crowd is moved by hate or by love, wonders, "And could politics ever be an expression of love?"

Against this quickly sketched backdrop, Ellison, as many interpreters have noted, targets several familiar but nonetheless valid foci of anticommunist criticism: the Brotherhood's belief that the people are a pliable mass, its compromises with white sensibilities (for example, in the design of the rainbow banner), its internally undemocratic structure, its betrayal of the Harlem work, and the theoretical root of these, its abstract and teleological view of history. Ellison further provides a gallery of Communist Party types: careerist, apologist for the changing party line, apparatchik (Wrestrum, Hambro, Jack). Though he also portrays honest, noncareerist Brotherhood members like brothers Maceo (chap. 23), Tarp, and Clifton, we learn little of their motivations. Most devastatingly, Ellison makes the protagonist himself the exemplar of a particular kind of second-rank Communist—both honest and self-deluded, his decent impulses compromised by an abstract ideology, deference to authority, and personal ambition, as when he is criticized and reassigned to lecture downtown (chap. 18): "[T]here was a logic in what he [Brother McAfee] said which I felt compelled to accept. . . . Now was certainly no time for inactivity. . . . [A]nd my main concern was to work my way ahead in the movement."

A young African American couple attends the National Communist Party Convention, held in New York City in May 1937. © Paul Dorsey/Time & Life Pictures/Getty Images.

World War II Changes the Brotherhood

With the Brotherhood's abandonment of its Harlem work (chaps. 20–23), *Invisible Man*'s focus broadens to include the issues posed by World War II. These chapters offer a recognizable though mythologized version of the CP's wartime turn, when, in the aftermath of Germany's invasion of the USSR (22 June 1941), the party moved from an antiwar to a fervently interventionist and win-the-war stance, backed [President Franklin Delano] Roosevelt's no-strike policy, and emphasized victory over fascism as its predominant goal. For at least part of this period, the *Daily Worker* carried the masthead slogan, "National Unity for Victory Over Nazi Enslavement." While trying to keep up work among African Americans, the party downplayed militant demands. "By the fall of 1941," [historian] Maurice Isserman's generally pro-CP study summarizes, "the Communists were arguing that a too militant defense of black rights at home would interfere with the war effort." The party's reversals with regard to [civil rights and labor activist] A. Philip Randolph's March On Washington movement for equal work in war industries (1941–43) were especially vivid. Ignoring the movement in its preparatory months (the first half of 1941), the *Daily Worker* offered a gingerly endorsement three weeks before the July 1 march date and attacked Randolph for calling off the march (June 25) when Roosevelt established the Fair Employment Practices Commission. But in the meantime the USSR had come into the war, and the Party's line gradually shifted to emphasizing Negro rights only in the context of the war effort. When Randolph organized follow-up rallies a year later in several cities, the *Daily Worker* initially branded them divisive. Ultimately, it covered New York's rally of 18,000 in Madison Square Garden a day late, applauding several speakers' "[s]plendid win-the-war addresses" but attacking as "insidious poison" the evening's high point, a dramatic sketch in which Canada Lee, as a Negro draftee, roused cheers and yells by declaring, "I'll fight Hitler, Mussolini, and the Japs all at the same time, but I'm telling you, I'll give those crackers down South the same damn medicine!"

Ellison's references to "sacrific[ing]" the Harlem members pursuant to an emphasis on "national and international" issues and "temporary alliances with other political groups" offer a recognizable version of this wartime shift. Recognizable, too, are some of the consequences—loss of members and the top officials' reversals of their previous positions. The protagonist's pained interview with Hambro may owe something to similar experiences of Richard Wright. The force of the protagonist's hopes, corrupted but also heightened by the sense of anticipating and controlling history, suggests the impact of the Brotherhood's betrayal: loss of confidence in an agency for a fraternal society.

In *Invisible Man*'s closing chapters and epilogue, . . . Ellison's protagonist grapples with this loss . . . [by dropping] a revolutionary standpoint in favor of one of long-term ameliorative struggle. . . . Like the portrayal of the Brotherhood, [this aspect] of *Invisible Man* [is] closely related to historical context, [specifically] the March On Washington and "double V" movements among African Americans during World War II.

The March movement, as already seen, waged an independent mass civil rights campaign in wartime; "double V" expressed the same idea. This slogan, usually said to have been introduced by the *Pittsburgh Courier* in February 1942, referred to victory against facism at home as well as abroad. Both crystallized an attitude popular among more militant African Americans—neither uncritically embracing the war effort, as urged by the Roosevelt administration and also the Communist Party, nor rejecting the war on pacifist or pro-Japanese grounds (each of which had some support) but supporting parallel struggles for war victory and for full, unconditional, and immediate civil rights in the US. These conceptions were a step away from the previous decade's alliance of African American leaders with Roosevelt and toward the start of an independent African American movement. . . . *Invisible Man*'s embodiment of the "double V" conception is the protagonist's reinterpretation of his grandfather's deathbed words. . . .

In answer to the riddle of what his grandfather meant by "overcome 'em with yeses," [Chapter 1], the protagonist has his first partial insight:

Could he have meant—hell, he must have meant the principle, that we were to affirm the principle on which the country was built and not the men, or at least not the men who did the violence. . . .

The protagonist is asking if it is possible to "overcome" this structure of entrenched power by affirming its face principles, and he understands for the first time that by "live with your head in the lion's mouth," his grandfather did not mean practicing a tricky accommodation but struggling for democratic principles so far as possible without self-destruction, as he had done in life. . . . "Overcome 'em with yesses" meant using "the principle" to overcome the oppressors.

The protagonist's . . . father asks,

"Or did he mean that we had to take the responsibility for all of it, for the men as well as the principle, because we were the heirs who must use the principle because no other fitted our needs?"

Finally, he asks . . .

Or was it, did he mean that "we should affirm the principle because we, through no fault of our own, were linked to all the others . . . who were tired of being the mere pawns in the futile game of 'making history?'"

Here "the principle" becomes nonracial and internationalist, focusing on the ties that African Americans . . . have or should have with "others," inferably both non–African Americans and non-Americans.

Ellison suggests an International commonality of interest that can use the democratic "principle" as a counterweight against Communist and non-Commmunist manipulators. Ellison further suggests that in this way African Americans may give leadership to the world's emergent peoples.

This three-part political meditation finds a metaphoric, quasi-mythic language for the "double V" conception of struggling for African American rights on the basis of US political beliefs and as an independent social movement, while taking this idea out of its wartime context and universalizing it as a response to oppression.

Foreseeing Changes in Culture

Invisible Man's historical roots help to explain some ambiguities of the novel's conclusion—between art and politics as modes of confronting the world, between goals of personal and social freedom, and between competing political and social blueprints for change. As those who follow critical discussions know, *Invisible Man* is often read as ending in confusion and exhaustion: "[T]he next step I couldn't make, so I've remained in the hole." What is sometimes wished away or seen as a formally unsatisfactory close can instead be viewed as an effort within a particular historical situation to see divergent potentialities for social activity and at least a possible future way forward. Both these aspects are intimately tied to the protagonist's just-enunciated conception of African Americans' relation to the United States and its political system, and in this sense the epilogue has a high degree of intellectual coherence. . . .

If *Invisible Man* has already described an expansive perspective of communal, and possibly multicommunal, struggle for democratic amelioration, this perspective has its own difficulties and contradictions. These too are part of *Invisible Man*'s reference to the specific situation of African American radicalism in the 1940s. . . .

These alternatives—limited autonomy in a restrictive society, democratic ameliorative struggle for "the principle," utopian struggle for a world of "Brotherhood"—were all inherent in the position of African Americans at the end of the period of radicalization in the 1930s and 1940s, on the eve of the renewed struggle of the later 1950s. These were and are, in fact, alternative possibilities for social action, and *Invisible Man* does not so much choose among them as record their existence. But while expressing these contradictory possibilities and the social stasis that partly conditions them, the novel also forecasts—necessarily provisionally and prospectively— the end of stasis. The Prologue's apothegm, "A hibernation is a covert preparation for a more overt action," and the Epilogue's promise, "I must emerge. . . . I'm coming out," prophesy—from darkness—what would appear in US social life only a few years later. Indeed, the change was already in the air. On 1 April 1952, just days before *Invisible Man's* 12 April publication, in one of four cases later consolidated as *Brown v. Board of Education*, Judge Collins J. Seitz ordered the integration of two Delaware schools, the first time any court had done so. . . .

Placed in the context of 1940's African American radicalism, *Invisible Man* loses none of its universal application. Indeed, arbitrary oppression, the emergence of "marginal" populations into historical action, the complex interplay of multiply defined identities, and the capacity, behind whatever mask of "invisibility," to dream the "ancient dreams" are among the most universal human experiences. But its contemporary contexts reveal *Invisible Man* as historically more specific, and incidentally more socially radical and prophetic, than do literary and cultural contexts alone. It is more historically specific because in addition to portraying an individual or even communal history in general terms, it also provides a mythic representation of African Americans' evolving sociopolitical commitments and ideology in two crucial periods of recent history. It is socially more radical because the concept of "affirm[ing] the principle," rather than appearing as an awkward bow to US ideals within an epilogue focused on personal and artistic autonomy, emerges as the novel's central strategic outlook, a logical culmination of the protagonist's and African Americans' experience of social struggle. This central conception, moreover, itself partly bridges the false divide between the novel's "political" and "universal" applications, because Ellison would view "affirm[ing] the principle," in its closeness to US reality and African American plebeian tradition, as the best available means by which to realize what Wright called "the inexpressibly human." Finally, *Invisible Man* is more socially prophetic because in addition to forecasting its hero's possible emergence as mature citizen and artist, it envisions African Americans' return to the center of national politics, and conceptualizes new methods of social action. Viewed against the backdrop of the history that shaped it, Ellison's novel gains the richness and concreteness of cultural and national history.

Ralph Ellison and the Mythology of Race

Jeff Abernathy

Jeff Abernathy is the president of Alma College, a private liberal arts institution in Michigan. He is the author of To Hell and Back: Race and Betrayal in the Southern Novel.

In the viewpoint below, Abernathy argues that Invisible Man *serves, in part, as Ellison's response to and ultimately his rewriting of the relationship between Huck Finn and the escaped slave Jim in Mark Twain's* Adventures of Huckleberry Finn, *a text that has served as a focal point for numerous African American authors. Abernathy argues that Ellison explores the fraudulent nature of white benevolence through seemingly well-meaning white characters who befriend the Invisible Man, only to eventually betray his trust. In this light, Huck Finn's benevolence toward Jim clearly holds no relevance to Ellison's narrator. Finally, Abernathy argues that Ellison's narrator attains an autonomy that goes beyond that of black characters in other southern novels. To reach this end, Ellison undermines racial stereotypes and allows his protagonist to grow through individualism rather than through racial unity.*

In her work on "racechange," [feminist literary critic] Susan Gubar writes of the means through which races come to know one another: "What one's imagination makes of other people is dictated, of course, by the laws of one's own personality and it is one of the ironies of black-white relations that, by means of what the white imagines the black man to be, the black man is enabled to know who the white man is." African American novelists have perceived the relationship between

Jeff Abernathy, *To Hell and Back: Race and Betrayal in the Southern Novel.* University of Georgia Press, 2003, pp. 128–130, 140–146. Copyright © 2003 by University of Georgia Press. All rights reserved. Reproduced by permission.

black and white from the vantage point of the subjugated. Since the emergence of the form from its early model of the slave narrative, they have frequently portrayed cross-racial relationships in which a black character guides a white companion toward moral development. A central moral imperative of the African American novel has naturally been an insistence that white Americans come to recognize the dissonance between the nation's professed ideals and its treatment of minorities. While [Mark Twain's] Huck Finn must first travel a thousand miles down the Mississippi River with Jim before he decides to "go to hell" rather than return Jim to slavery, Bigger Thomas recognizes the moral inequity present in his society from the beginning of Richard Wright's *Native Son*. The ways in which blacks cope with that inequity provide the locus of the African American novel, a genre that, as Arnold Rampersad has argued, looks back time and again to *Huckleberry Finn* as both source and foil.

The Theme of Racial Identity

The language of white culture necessarily brings with it that culture's essentializing structures, and African American writers of the twentieth century attempted to undo such structures even as the language they used expressed them. [Critic] Henry Louis Gates argues that the struggle black writers have with the very language they use leads them to employ the traditions of an African heritage; these writers, Gates suggests, "speak in standard Romance or Germanic languages and literary structures, but almost always speak with a distinct and resonant accent, an accent that signifies (upon) the various black vernacular literary traditions, which are still being written down." It is a duality that frustrates even as it liberates, fractures even as it joins.

Racial identity appears as central theme time and again in the fiction of African American writers from Charles Chesnutt to Randall Kenan, just as we have found it to be central to the work of white writers in the South. African American writers have of course themselves struggled with the stereotypes placed upon blacks by white culture. Jean Toomer and Chesnutt, both of whom could have passed as "white," made conscious choices to "remain" black rather than pass, and they narrate similar experiences in their fiction. Describing the period in which he wrote *Cane*, Toomer asserted that his "need for artistic expression has pulled me deeper and deeper into the Negro group. As my powers of receptivity increased, I found myself loving it in a way that I could never love the other." This intriguing consideration—*whiteness* as otherness—emerges powerfully in Toomer's work, and we see African American writers exploring just such possibilities as they adapt the pattern of reversal we've found since Twain.

Here I examine the ways in which . . . Ralph Ellison, respond[s] to, signif[ies] upon, and finally rewrite[s] the relationship between Huck Finn and Jim. [His] protagonist work[s] against the negative self-definition placed upon [him] by the white South. In portraying [an] autonomous black character removed from the essentializing structures of the white southern novel, [Ellison] repudiate[s] not Twain's text, where [he] plainly find[s] inspiration, but the powerful recoiling from black identity to be found there. If the white characters here rarely resemble Huck Finn in their social standing, they do, like Huck, look to the black protagonist . . . for either clemency or redemption. [Ellison] portray[s] the inherent condescension and manipulation of a white character who seeks false refuge in blackness in broad caricature. Having gained the perspective of their black protagonist, these white characters answer in multiple means the question [early twentieth-century black intellectual] W.E.B. DuBois claimed the "other world," the white world, asked of him indirectly but interminably: "How does it feel to be a problem?" . . .

Race Made Visible

The twelve years between the publication of [Richard Wright's] *Native Son* (1940) and Ralph Ellison's *Invisible Man* (1952) saw the end of World War Two and the emergence of a new consciousness among African Americans with the return of black veterans who had not only fought for their country but also witnessed a world beyond the Jim Crow [overtly segregated] South or the equally segregated North.

Ellison's novel is, like Wright's, a meditation on African American migration but one that takes a wry look at the emergence of labor consciousness and the political movements of the 1930s. While Wright wrote a stark and severe critique of American culture, Ellison protests that culture with one hand and celebrates it with the other, even turning frequently to mock the nature of protest itself. Ellison's narrator, as critic Michael Kreyling argues, "sees protest as yet another co-optation into white-determined identity." And Ellison's view of himself as modernist writer, as critic, prevented him from writing out of the tradition of African American protest: "[W]hen we approach contemporary writing from the perspective of segregation, as is commonly done by sociologically-minded thinkers, we automatically limit ourselves to one external aspect of a complex whole, which leaves one little to say concerning its personal, internal elements."

Ellison casts his nets wide in the novel, and it would be reductive to suggest that his book signifies solely on Mark Twain's *Huck Finn*: Ellison's book is a rich response to the whole of American literature. But Ellison himself described the signal role that Twain's book plays in the culture: "No Huck and Jim, no American novel as we know it." And thirty years after the publication of *Invisible Man*, he acknowledged that a primary purpose had been to meditate on the rhetorical and intellectual division of black and white:

> So my task was one of revealing the human universals hidden within the plight of one who was both black and Ameri-

can, and not only as a means of conveying my personal vision of possibility, but as a way of dealing with the sheer
rhetorical challenge involved in communicating across our
barriers of race and religion, class, color and region—barriers which consist of the many strategies of division that
were designed, and still function, to prevent what would
otherwise have been a more or less natural recognition of
the reality of black and white fraternity. . . . Most of all, I
would have to approach racial stereotypes as a given fact of
the social process and proceed, while gambling with the
reader's capacity for fictional truth, to reveal the human
complexity which stereotypes are intended to conceal.

Fraudulent Benevolence

Like Wright, Ellison examines in part the fraudulent nature of
white benevolence. Ellison persistently contests the sincerity of
professed goodwill on the part of whites toward his black
characters. The narrator's repeated encounters with whites
who claim generosity as their motivation leave him convinced
they are unable to conceive of their relationships with him in
anything but essentialized terms. Their generosity emerges as
a form of loathing.

In the second chapter of *Invisible Man*, Ellison looks to
Twain's paradigm in joining his narrator with Mr. Norton, a
benefactor of the college that so closely resembles Ellison's
own Tuskegee Institute. The narrator chauffeurs Norton
through the countryside surrounding the college, a role that
emphasizes his servility in deference to this white philanthropist. Norton's claim that his own fate is bound together with
the narrator's, which comes as he heaps commands upon the
narrator, urges reconsideration of Twain's model: "'So you see,
young man, you are involved in my life quite intimately, even
though you've never seen me before. You are bound to a great
dream and to a beautiful monument. If you become a good
farmer, a chef, a preacher, doctor, singer, mechanic—whatever
you become, and even if you fail, you are my fate. And you

Still from a 1960 film adaptation of Adventures of Huckleberry Finn, *starring Eddie Hodges (left) as Huck Finn and Archie Moore as Jim.* © Grey Villet/Time & Life Pictures/ Getty Images.

must write me and tell me the outcome.'" We have seen before white characters whose "fate" is bound up with a black companion. Ellison parodies the notion that white characters might achieve wholeness through a vision of their own participation in a black world, through their resultant confrontation with the guilt that haunts them and white America. Norton's plea for racial innocence is much like that of Wright's Mr. Dalton, but Ellison renders such a proposition absurd. The "dream" to which the narrator is "bound" is one that has the familiar result of lashing blacks to subservient roles, as we see in the Golden Day, a bar in which Norton and the narrator encounter the "veterans," former black professionals for whom aspiration will always exceed rank. Likewise, the "monument," a campus statue professedly depicting the college founder removing the veil from kneeling students (but that the narrator suspects may instead depict the securing of the veil), calls to mind the national monument for which the narrator will later mix drops of black paint into buckets of white paint, blackness into a sea of white. The narrator eventually sees just how superficial—and outrageous—Norton's claim to moral kinship is. And even as he claims such connection, Norton of course retains his own patriarchal identity and power.

The Collective African American Identity

Throughout the text, the narrator points to the irony of Norton's presumptions through his own naive response. "'*You* are important because if you fail *I* have failed by one individual, one defective cog,'" Norton claims (ironically tying the narrator's individuality to a "cog," which has none), to which the narrator thinks in response, "But you don't even know my name." The narrator forms such fleeting relationships with white characters throughout *Invisible Man*, compelling him to see that white American society persistently appropriates what narrow identity it has allowed him. While the narrator cannot see himself as Jim, as a one-dimensional minstrel figure, the white characters around him persist in asking him to assume such a role. In *Invisible Man*, Ellison exposes the failings not only of the social conscience of white America but also of the literary relationships exemplifying that conscience.

Ellison's literary allusions are quite direct in the narrator's relationship with the son of the elusive Mr. Emerson. The narrator seeks a patron in the senior Mr. Emerson, but the younger intervenes, ostensibly to warn the narrator of his college president's duplicity in sending him north with no hope of employment. We soon discover the younger Emerson to be an aspiring Huck to the narrator's Jim, however, and Ellison references Twain's text to demonstrate how flawed the relationship finally is:

> "Look," he said, his face working violently, "I was trying to tell you that I know many things about you—not you personally, but fellows like you. Not much, either, but still more than the average. With us it's still Jim and Huck Finn. . . . Please don't misunderstand me; I don't say all this to impress you. Or to give myself some kind of sadistic catharsis. Truly, I don't. But I do know this world you're trying to contact—all its virtues and all its unspeakables—Ha, yes, unspeakables. I'm afraid my father considers *me* one of the unspeakables. . . . I'm Huckleberry, you see."

[Writer] Alan Nadel observes that Emerson's declaration— "'I'm Huckleberry'"—immediately tips off the reader to his duplicity: the only character in Twain's novel to use Huck's full name is Miss Watson, who represents hypocritical religious fervor and ignorance. But the narrator will in any case have no such identity put upon him: "He laughed drily as I tried to make sense of his ramblings. *Huckleberry*? Why did he keep talking about that kid's story?"

The narrator will not allow Emerson to plead "innocence" à la Huck Finn: "'Aren't you curious about what lies behind the face of things?'" Emerson asks. "'Yes, sir, but I'm mainly interested in a job,'" the narrator replies. The narrator consciously rejects the white liberal's perception of the relationship between well-meaning whites and destitute blacks. Huck Finn's tale, appealing as it has been to the southern novelist, holds no relevance for Ralph Ellison's narrator.

Ellison Undermines Stereotypes

Late in the novel, Ellison's portrayal of Sybil, the white woman who attempts to seduce the narrator, reveals the writer's outright rejection of white condescension. As in the earlier scenes, Ellison undermines the role of the white benefactor by reducing it to the absurd. Sybil claims that she wants the narrator to rape her because she has always heard that this is what black men do to white women: "'Well ever since I first heard about it, even when I was a very little girl, I've wanted it to happen to me.'" The narrator back-pedals from the advance of yet another white character who has invested in a blackness that never existed. Like the younger Emerson, Sybil assumes the existence of a trust that the narrator will not enter into because of the condescension and stereotype it implies: Sybil imagines a familiar bond with the narrator, but Ellison makes clear that any such bond is based upon an essentialized view of blacks on the part of whites. The narrator rejects Sybil's proposal outright: when he leaves her lying unconscious in her apartment, the narrator scrawls a message on Sybil's body—"SYBIL YOU WERE RAPED BY SANTA CLAUS"—that demonstrates his recognition of the absurdity implicit in Sybil's fantasy of black behavior: the myth she believes is as false as the myth of Santa Claus. Like Wright before him, Ellison chooses the ultimate taboo of southern society—sex between a black man and a white woman—to undermine the stereotypes of that society.

In these few encounters, as in his encounters with the many African American characters who expect him to act in keeping with their racial expectations throughout the novel, Ellison's narrator elects to set his own course rather than allow another to set it for him. Neither will he assume the responsibility of being the "fate" of another. At the end, he concludes that he must stake out his own identity, free of the expectations both the white and black communities place upon him: "I had no longer to run for or from the Jacks and the Emersons and the Bledsoes and Nortons, but only from their confusion, impatience, and refusal to recognize the beautiful absurdity of their American identity and mine. . . . I knew that it was better to live out one's own absurdity than to die for that of others, whether for Ras's or Jack's." The narrator asserts a role for blackness in the American identity, a conclusion that white protagonists have arrived at often enough but one from which they have so often retreated. For Ellison's narrator, that identity is not one of racial unity but instead of individualism, much like that which Huck Finn claims for himself at the end of Twain's novel. In the end, the narrator requires no validating presence at all: he has attained the autonomy that Bigger Thomas was striving for and that Jim and his literary descendants never obtain. For Ellison, individual identity comes not directly from external relationships but instead from one's internal response to them. In claiming an autonomy for his black protagonist beyond that attained by the black characters in the southern novel, Ellison repudiates the mythmaking of *Huck Finn*.

Striving Toward a Black Democratic Individuality in *Invisible Man*

Jack Turner

Jack Turner is assistant professor of political science at the University of Washington. His research focuses on American political thought, race in American politics, and liberal democratic theory.

In this viewpoint, Turner argues that Ellison's central metaphor of invisibility in Invisible Man *applies generally to all Americans. Americans do not know themselves, Turner says, because, like Ellison's protagonist, they bury their historical truths and present realities underground. By illuminating what he has buried, the Invisible Man comes to an understanding of his own experiences, Turner argues. He finds freedom within segregation through the narrative act of transforming experience into meaning. In doing so, Turner says, the Invisible Man becomes a model of democratic individuality: he engages history, confronts the legacies of slavery, exposes the illusions of white supremacy, and acts politically on behalf of democracy. Turner argues that* Invisible Man *introduces the idea of interracial fraternity and suggests that African Americans can save America from self-destruction through forsaking claims to retribution and superiority and embracing democratic individuality.*

The most significant way [Ralph] Ellison frees democratic individuality from its parochial white moorings is through his virtuosic 1952 novel *Invisible Man*. *Invisible Man* is the story of an African American male journeying toward self-knowledge after he is expelled from college in the Deep South and goes north to Harlem to redeem himself. Striving for respectability, the unnamed protagonist travels to New York under the impression that he will be able to win readmission to the college after a stint of work for one of the trustees. Yet he is disabused of this notion soon after arriving. On visiting the office of a prospective employer—ironically named Mr. Emerson—the protagonist learns that he has been sent down a blind alley. The college president who promised to give the Invisible Man a second chance has sabotaged him through a poison-pen letter of introduction. This is the first of many moments of disillusionment for the protagonist. Throughout the novel he tries to achieve respectability and social visibility by pursuing preset paths of success. Each moment of disillusionment imparts greater knowledge; at the same time, his disillusionment occurs in fits and starts. Only after assuming several different social vocations and identities does he realize that the burden of freedom and individuality begins and ends with him; no social station or vocation can give his life stable meaning. Every individual is alone in deciding his identity. The self is a process and "Nothing is for keeps."

Finding Freedom Through Narration

Invisible Man, however, is more than an existential quest for selfhood. Its setting within the racially segregated United States of the interwar period allows Ellison to probe the ways white supremacy distorts Americans' perceptions of themselves. Its central metaphor of invisibility applies not just to the social state of its central character, but to the American individual generally. We do not know ourselves, Ellison implies, because we bury so much of our history and the truth of present reality underground. Fittingly, the Invisible Man narrates his journey from New York's underground—a cellar illuminated with electricity he steals from "Monopolated Light & Power." Only by illuminating the underground can the narrator understand his American experience. Imbued with an evolving appreciation of false consciousness, the Invisible Man analyzes it in the Emersonian language [in the style of philosopher and writer Ralph Waldo Emerson] of sleep, dream, and illusion. Soon after a disillusioning experience midway through the novel, the protagonist returns to his New York hotel and surveys the reign of illusion among his black compatriots:

> The moment I entered the . . . lobby of Men's House I was overcome by a sense of alienation and hostility. . . . I knew that I could live there no longer, that that phase of my life was past. The lobby was the meeting place for various groups still caught up in the illusions that had just been boomeranged out of my head: college boys working to return to school down South; older advocates of racial progress with Utopian schemes for building black business empires; preachers ordained by no authority except their own . . . community "leaders" without followers; old men of sixty or more still caught up in post–Civil War dreams of freedom within segregation; the pathetic ones who possessed nothing beyond their dreams of being gentlemen, who held small jobs or drew small pensions, and all pretending to be engaged in some vast, though obscure, enterprise . . . [the] crowd for whom I now felt a contempt such as only a disillusioned dreamer feels for those still unaware that they dream . . .

Freedom within segregation is a dream, the narrator suggests. This claim is surprising, given that the narrator is realizing freedom within segregation through narration. Narration allows him to transform experience into meaning, to objectify his subjectivity on the written page. Is there not freedom in creativity? Even if the narrator grants this, he implies that expressive freedom is not enough. The narrator calls his time underground a "hibernation" and defines hibernation as "a covert preparation for a more overt action." The Invisible Man plans to leave his hole "when the moment for action presents itself." The ultimate reason he has reflected on his experience and distilled its meaning is for action's sake. "Without the possibility of action, all knowledge comes to one labeled 'file and forget,'" he declares, "and I can neither file nor forget."

A Strategy for Democracy

Ellison's Invisible Man models a type of democratic individuality designed to engage history's shadow, to confront the ways racial slavery and its legacies distort American character, to explode the illusions white supremacy imposes on all citizens, and to act politically on behalf of transracial democracy. Specially fitted for the hall of mirrors that is American modernity, his psychological liberation comes when he claims the right to tell the meaning of his experience. This episode occurs near the end of the novel when he realizes that the interracial social democratic "Brotherhood" of which he had been spokesman was selling out its Negro constituency to advance other aims:

> I leaned against a stone wall along the park . . . and shook with rage. It was all a swindle, an obscene swindle! They had set themselves up to describe the world. What did they know of us, except that we numbered so many, worked on certain jobs, offered so many votes, and provided so many marchers for some protest parade of theirs? I leaned there, aching to humiliate them, to refute them. And now all past humiliations became precious parts of my experience, and for the first time . . . I began to accept my past and, as I accepted it, I felt memories welling up within me. It was as though I'd learned suddenly to look around corners; images of past humiliations flickered through my head and I saw that they were more than separate experiences. They were me; they defined me. I was my experiences and my experiences were me, and no blind men . . . could take that, or change one single itch, taunt, laugh, cry, scar, ache, rage or pain of it.

The protagonist claims the right to describe the world as he sees it, even if it upends the descriptions of others. He gives new meaning to Emersonian self-trust by deploying it against white ideological hegemony. He realizes that aspects of his history which were once sources of shame—his family's roots in slavery, his grandfather's insistence that he had "been a traitor all [his] born days," the cryptic deathbed advice his grandfather gave him to "Live with your head in the lion's mouth . . . overcome 'em with yeses, undermine 'em with grins, agree 'em to death and destruction"—are resources for living, as well as for achieving American democracy. By story's end, he discerns the way his grandfather, an "old slave," had sketched a strategy for realizing American democracy:

> Could he have meant—hell, he *must* have meant the principle, that we were to affirm the principle on which the country was built and not the men, or at least not the men who did the violence. Did he mean say "yes" because he knew that the principle was greater than the men, greater than the numbers and the vicious power and all the methods used to corrupt its name? . . . Or did he mean that we have to take the responsibility for all of it, for the men as well as the principle, because we were their heirs who must use the principle because no other fitted our needs? . . . Was it that we of all, we, most of all, had to affirm the principle, the plan in whose name we had been brutalized and sacrificed . . . because we were older than they, in the sense of what it took to live in the world with others . . . [?]

> "Agree 'em to death and destruction," grandfather had advised. Hell, weren't they their own death and their own destruction except as the principle lived in them and in us? And here's the cream of the joke: Weren't we *part of them* as well as apart from them and subject to die when they died?

Ellison makes black people democracy's final trustee. Black citizens will realize American democracy by insisting—even in the face of white resistance and violence—that all men are created equal and entitled to life, liberty, and the pursuit of happiness. More importantly, African Americans will save America from self-destruction by accepting their oppressors as fellow citizens and moral equals, forsaking claims to retribution and superiority. History teaches that whites are their own death and destruction "except as the principle live[s] in them and in us." Likewise, black people would be their own death and destruction if they sought not equality and justice but merely an inversion of American racial hierarchy. Black and white Americans, furthermore, are indivisible: "they" are part of "us" and "we" are part of "them." As he reflects on equality and liberty, Ellison introduces the idea of fraternity—specifically, the reality of American interracial fraternity: the kind [novelist] James Baldwin spoke of when he wrote to his nephew,

> But these men are your brothers—your lost, younger brothers. And if the word *integration* means anything, this is what it means: that we, with love, shall force our brothers to see themselves as they are, to cease fleeing from reality and begin to change it. . . .

Toward a Broader Democratic Individuality

In his life as a public intellectual, Ellison took up the moral quest he imputed to the Invisible Man at the novel's end. Though he often insisted that his primary vocation was artist—not political leader—Ellison could not help but imbue his art with a strong political dimension. *Invisible Man*, after all, left its hero contemplating going aboveground to act on behalf of "the principle." The entire context of Ellison's art and criticism, America's racial division, had politics at its core. On accepting the National Book Award for *Invisible Man* in 1953, he declared that the "chief significance of *Invisible Man* as a fiction . . . [is] its attempt to return to the mood of personal moral responsibility for democracy. . . ." But before America can achieve democracy, it must achieve a keener sense of reality. Because the artist's task is to capture reality as fully and faithfully as possible, the vocations of artist and political actor merge. Despite his frequent insistence on the autonomy of art from politics, *Invisible Man* was a political act on Ellison's own terms. If we read *Invisible Man* together with both Ellison's voluminous social and cultural criticism and his posthumous novel *Juneteenth* (1999), we can identify at least two political intellectual projects at work. The first is diagnostic: identifying the individual and social psychoses underlying American white supremacy. Ellison seeks to instill in "American democratic individualism" an awareness of the motive forces of white supremacy and of the ways they distort American character and perception; he seeks especially to attune the white American individual to those aspects of reality he has historically evaded and those injustices he has habitually ignored. Ellison's second project is reconstructive: imagining new metaphors for American experience that can help citizens see their siblings across the color line and appreciate the mongrel nature of their identities. Here Ellison provides Americans with the imaginative equipment they need to escape racialized social outlooks and see the world from the perspective of racial others. If citizens can assimilate these metaphors, they will enhance their capacities for multiple perspectivism, and in so doing, see a more vast reality. Through these two projects, Ellison broadens the perspective of Emersonian democratic individuality.

Ralph Ellison's Literary Pursuit of Racial Justice

Thomas S. Engeman

Thomas S. Engeman is associate professor of political science at Loyola University Chicago. He is coauthor of The Presidency and Political Science: Two Hundred Years of Constitutional Debate.

In the following viewpoint, Engeman follows the Invisible Man's personal journey toward racial justice, a path laid by the Declaration of Independence's principles of equality and liberty. While the Invisible Man escapes the hypocrisy of the South, Engeman explains that the protagonist discovers a similar model of hypocrisy in the North when he works for the Liberty Paint company. The Invisible Man is hopeful of finding liberation, but he remains oppressed at his job. When he joins the Brotherhood, he gains a voice as a spokesperson for the party, only to later feel betrayed by the group when it deliberately provokes riots in Harlem for its own political gain. Engeman argues that the riots give the Invisible Man insight into the virtues of urban blacks and free him from his illusions about racial justice and liberation.

More than most major writers, in numerous essays and speeches, Ralph Ellison steadily commented on the importance of literature for life, and the principles of American democracy for racial justice. Because *Invisible Man* ... [is a] "novel of ideas," a brief introduction to Ellison's reflections on literature and democracy will prepare us for a study of racial justice in the novel.

While often deploying the pyrotechnics of surrealism, including extended dream sequences and wild comic conceits, Ralph Ellison argued the goal of his writing is literary realism:

Thomas S. Engeman, *Ralph Ellison and the Raft of Hope: A Political Companion to Invisible Man.* University Press of Kentucky, 2004, pp. 91–98. All rights reserved. Reproduced by permission of The University Press of Kentucky.

> [W]hat one listens for in a novel: the degree to which it contains what Henry James termed "felt life," . . . that quality conveyed by the speaker's knowledge and feeling for the regional, racial, religious, and class unities and differences within the land, and his awareness of the hopes and values of a diverse people struggling to achieve the American promise in their own time, in their own place, and with the means at hand.

Unlike his "enemy" the social scientist, the writer invents images to capture the world's complex reality. Literature best reveals the possibilities of human knowledge and action; art must be a guide for "ordinary" experience:

> But hope and aspiration are indeed important aspects of the reality of Negro American history, no less than that of others. Besides, it's one of our roles as writers to remind ourselves of such matters, just as it is to make assertions tempered by the things of the spirit. It might sound arrogant to say so, but writers and poets help create or reveal hidden realities by asserting their existence. . . .
>
> I do not find it a strain to point to the heroic component of our experience, for these seem truths which we have long lived by, but which we must now recognize consciously.

Knowledge of the literary classics elevates social science's negative realism: "We (Negroes) depend upon outsiders—mainly sociologists—to interpret our lives for us. It doesn't seem to occur to us that our interpreters might well be not so much prejudiced as ignorant, insensitive, and arrogant. It doesn't occur to us that they might be of shallow personal culture, or innocent of the complexities of actual living." In artistically reconstructing the world, writers must inspire it with their greater understanding of human possibility: "You must pay the Negro community the respect of trying to see it through the enriching perspectives provided by great literature, using your own intelligence to make up for the differences. . . . Human beings are basically the same and differ mainly in lifestyle. Here revelation is called for, not argument."

Defending the Declaration of Independence

Ellison also maintains the importance of the [of Independence's] principles of equality and liberty for racial justice. These principles were mainly embodied in the Constitution and later refined by Abraham Lincoln. He referred to this nearly sacred trinity as "the framers of Declaration, the Constitution, and Lincoln."

> [T]he Declaration of Independence marked the verbalization of our colonial forefathers' intentions of disposing of the king's authority. . . . The Constitution marked the gloriously optimistic assertion and legitimization of a new form of authority and the proclaiming of a new set of purposes and promises. . . . Through the dramatic conflict of democratic society, it would seek to fulfill its revolutionary assertions.

> We made a formulation here of what we were and who we were, and what we expected to be, and we wrote it down in the documents of the Bill of Rights, the Constitution, the Declaration of Independence. I mean that we put ourselves on the books as to what we were and would become, and we were stuck with it. And we were stuck with it partially through a process of deification which came through the spilling of blood and through the sacrifices which were endured. . . .

Ellison also admired the "agonistic . . . conflict of democratic society." Competition results in a creative society in all fields; Americans, thus, recreate themselves through the revolutionary principles of the Declaration. . . .

A life-long defender of the Declaration's color-blind teaching of equality and individual liberty, Ellison was highly critical of Black liberation movements, illustrated in *Invisible Man* by the Black Nationalist Ras's politics of race and violence:

"Brothers are the same color; how the hell you call these white men *brother*? . . . We sons of Mama Africa, you done forgot? You black, Black! . . . They hate you, mahn. You African. AFRICAN! . . . They sell you out. . . . They enslave us— you forget that? How can they mean a black mahn any good?"

For Ellison, Ras's racial nationalism revives the recently buried specter of Nazism, and, ultimately, of white racial superiority as the justification for slavery:

The Germany which produced Beethoven and Hegel and Mann turned its science and technology to the monstrous task of genocide; one hopes that when what are known as "Negro" societies are in full possession of the world's knowledge and in control of their destinies, they will bring to an end all those savageries which for centuries have been committed in the name of race. From what we are witnessing in certain parts of the world today, however, there is no guarantee that simply being non-white offers any guarantee of this. The demands of state policy are apt to be more influential than morality.

Therefore, liberal principles—guaranteeing opportunity, but demanding excellence—offer the only safe basis for liberation:

Democracy is a collectivity of individuals.

The great writers of the nineteenth century and the best of the twentieth have always reminded us that the business of being an American is an arduous task, as Henry James said, and it requires constant attention to our consciousness and conscientiousness. The law ensures the conditions, the stage upon which we act; the rest of it is up to the individual.

But the individual liberation explored in *Invisible Man* is hostile to the kind of fellow feeling and social knowledge required to help liberate others. Indeed, the existential search for self-knowledge through a flight to solitude appears altogether hostile to society. The invisible man's existential "visibility" first appears in isolation from society: his family, college, political party, and work. . . .

Invisible Man seeks individual liberation through freedom from social oppression. "Invisible man," or IM, like [German philosopher Friedrich] Nietzsche's [prophet] Zarathustra, finds freedom from "the flies of the market-place" only in solitude. After leaving his family, IM eventually escapes the racism of Southern and Northern life altogether. Invisible in racist America, he gains the "visible" he craves by living alone, under the crowded streets of New York.

Ellison Embraces Du Bois's Themes

Invisible Man's exploration of race relations is similar to [early twentieth-century black intellectual] W.E.B. Du Bois's *The Souls of Black Folk*. (The other common theme of these works is pessimism about piercing the Veil, breaching the color line, of racial segregation.) The differences between the two works are also instructive. Du Bois mainly wrote vignettes in his own name, while Ellison's nameless IM is a purely literary creation. Moreover, the subtleties and humor of IM's quixotic quest go far beyond Du Bois's sociological essays.

Nevertheless, *Invisible Man* and *The Souls of Black Folk* share many themes: (1) the insufficiency of Booker T. Washington's accommodationism; (2) the pervasiveness of racism in both the North and South; (3) the centrality of music in Negro culture; and, most significantly, (4) the "double sightedness" of Black existence, causing Black invisibility. Du Bois observes:

> The Negro is a sort of seventh son, born with a veil, and gifted with second-sight in this American world—a world which yields him no true self-consciousness, but only lets him see himself through the revelation of the other world. It is a peculiar sensation, this double-consciousness, this sense

of always looking at one's self through the eyes of others, of measuring one's soul by the tape of a world that looks on in amused contempt and pity.

Invisible Man explores the effects of Du Bois's double consciousness on Blacks. But all Americans are enslaved by race prejudice. Regarding his writing, Ellison said: "I will not ignore the racial dimensions at all, but I will try to put them into a human perspective." He added, "For it is our fate as Americans [white and Negro] to achieve that sense of self-consciousness through our own efforts." Therefore, he insists on the origin of *Invisible Man* in Fyodor Dostoevsky's philosophical *Notes from Underground*, not the political/racial writings of Richard Wright's *Native Son* and Du Bois's *Souls of Black Folk*.

While racism *is* the reality IM overcomes to obtain self-conscious freedom, every human is similarly fated to illusion and oppression. IM learns that Reverend Homer Barbee, the blind seer of his beloved College, is both physically *and* intellectually blind to the difference between illusion and reality. Jack, the glass-eyed leader of the "Brotherhood," has become blind to the meaning of justice. If IM eventually triumphs over his social blindness, attaining a rare liberation, he remains uncertain how his new knowledge can be used to destroy racism and segregation.

IM grows up in the rural, segregated South. With one exception, his family comprises "good Negroes," followers of Booker T. Washington. They believe personal honesty, hard work, and ability are rewarded in America. "[T]hey were told they were free, united with others of our country in everything pertaining to the common good, and, in everything social, separate like the fingers of the hand. And they believed it. They exulted in it. They stayed in their place [and] worked hard." The exception to the family's foolish docility is IM's grandfather, who believes "our life is a war." He teaches them to "live with your head in the lion's mouth. I want you to

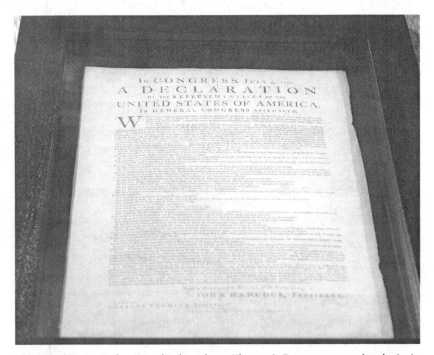

The United States Declaration of Independence. Thomas S. Engeman argues that the Invisible Man's pursuit of racial justice is informed by the principles outlined in this foundational document. © L. Cohen/WireImage/Getty Images.

overcome them with yeses, undermine 'em with grins, agree 'em to death and destruction, let 'em swoller you till they vomit or bust wide open." This unfathomable call to arms remains the central and "constant puzzle" for IM; it is so opposed to every view of race taught him by whites and Negroes alike. He soon learns that in searching for the liberating truth, he finds himself "carrying out his advice in spite of myself."

If comically told, the racial landscape Ellison paints is uniformly bleak. The only aid crossing the color line comes from a gay man who helps the hero as an act of revenge against his father. Moreover, in racist America influential Negroes become agents of oppression. IM's greatest enemy is President Bledsoe, the hypocritical successor of his College's benevolent Founder (a Booker T. Washington–like figure).

The Path of Racism

The novel opens with a display of overt racism in IM's small southern town. The white leaders' monthly "smoker" features various adult entertainments. Prominent among them is a free-for-all with local black "boys." The top graduate of the colored high school, IM discovers he must first brawl in the "battle royal" before presenting his honorific address, and receiving their award for his achievement. Speaking through his bloodied mouth, IM repeats the accepted views of voluntary segregation presented by Booker T. Washington at the Atlanta Exposition. Receiving the whites' praise as a "boy" who will "some day lead his people in the proper paths," IM gladly accepts their scholarship to Bledsoe's college, which will "encourage him in the right direction."

The sterile Tuskegee-like college *appears* a model of Booker T. Washington's benevolent ideal of progress through education, although it proves only an empire of illusion and tyranny. The college corrupts students by demanding they accept segregation, and their own inferiority, enabling their oppressor, President Bledsoe, to become wealthy and honored. A realist, Bledsoe tells IM the stark truth: "Well, that's the way it is. It's a nasty deal and I don't always like it myself. But you listen to me: I didn't make it, and I know that I can't change it. But I've made my place in it, and I'll have every Negro in the country hanging on tree limbs by morning if it means staying where I am."

The College presents a sanitized view of Negro life to attract the support of its idealistic white benefactors. Donors pay the college to atone for the exploitation of Negroes in their northern factories. Unwilling to seek racial justice in the North, the trustees willingly accept Bledsoe's comfortable vision of racial decorum and progress. The students dutifully play the game, appearing to conform to the strict ideals of a New England education.

The collegians are forbidden contact with the inmates of a local insane asylum. IM learns why when forced to take a Trustee to a black brothel when the inmates are there. Educated black war veterans, who treat whites as their equals, they have been committed for their insane lack of social awareness. For exposing the College's ridiculous racial tableaus, IM is permanently exiled.

Still believing in Bledsoe's goodness, IM accepts his letters of introduction to the College's wealthy New York friends. After inexplicable failures, he learns the letters are not those of grace. Recipients are encouraged to deceive IM about the College's willingness to help him, or permit his return:

> Thus, while the bearer is no longer a member of our scholastic family, it is highly important that his severance with the college be executed as painlessly as possible. I beg of you, sir, to help him continue in the direction of that promise which, like the horizon, recedes ever brightly and distantly beyond the hopeful traveler.

IM reformulates the letter's message: "The Robin bearing this letter is a former student. Please hope him to death, and keep him running."

The Invisible Man Believes in Liberation

Having escaped the total racism and hypocrisy of Southern society, in the North IM tries his luck at Liberty Paint, manufacturer of the purest paint made in America. "Optic White" is used by the (still segregated) United States Government; "Keep America Pure with Liberty Paints" is the company's (and the Government's) motto. Lucius Brockway, the old defender of the company's paternal racial order, wrote the company's tag line: "If It's Optic White, It's the Right White." He has made the Negro slogan *pay*: "If you're white, you're right." IM is made Brockway's assistant, working the basement boilers brewing the "base" for the greatest white "covering" in the world. Lucius cynically brags: "Our white is so white you can paint a

95

chunka coal and you'd have to crack it open with a sledge hammer to prove it wasn't white clear through."

IM becomes the catalyst for the plant's racial conflicts. The white boss considers Negroes incompetent, but is unable to instruct IM in mixing the hard white paint. Since young Negro college students, like IM, are hired to replace more highly paid whites, the union members believe he is a management fink, and "undeveloped" as a worker. The third camp are Negroes like Brockway, who, like President Bledsoe, have made the system work for them and will now "hang from a tree" any agents of change. When the hero tells Brockway he accidentally attended a union meeting, the latter explodes: "I knowed you belonged to that bunch of troublemaking foreigners! I knowed it! Git out! . . . Git out of my basement!" When IM refuses to give him his personal allegiance, Brockway blows up a boiler in revenge. In the plant's infirmary, the white medical staff employ a new electric lobotomy machine to cure the hero's antisocial rebelliousness. Once again, IM remains oppressed and invisible to the warring racial forces, but ever optimistic, he still believes there is an accepted way to pass through the Veil to liberation and "visibility."

IM's turn to political leadership is prepared through his friendship with his landlady, Mary Rambo. Mary thinks Negroes no longer require the economic enlightenment and moral uplift of Booker T. Washington, but the leadership of W.E.B. Du Bois's "Talented Tenth," and the NAACP [National Association for the Advancement of Colored People]. Breaking down legal barriers, a new Negro elite will liberate the black masses. IM finds living with Mary pleasant, "except for her constant talk about leadership and responsibility. . . . Mary reminded me constantly that something was expected of me, some act of leadership, some newsworthy achievement." But it is only a small step from Du Bois's elitist democracy to the violence of the Brotherhood's warlike Party.

A brilliant speaker, IM is drafted into the (Communistic) Brotherhood to be its Harlem spokesman. He soon begins to question the Brotherhood's authoritarianism. Suppressing his doubts, IM stays with the Brotherhood until convinced belatedly of its indifference to Negroes. In the face of the Black Nationalist Ras's opposition, IM builds the Party in Harlem, only to be suddenly removed. Ras rapidly increases his agitation, causing Harlem to erupt in violence. IM understands the Brotherhood deliberately caused the riot; it was ordered by "Moscow." By showing American racism to the world, the riot was intended to checkmate American foreign policy. "I could see it now, see it clearly and in growing magnitude. It [the riot] was not suicide, but murder. The committee had planned it."

But the great riot reveals aspects of humanity obscure in peace. Once liberated, the Negro "masses" demonstrate genuine virtues. Remarkably courageous, they have a genuine sense of community and organizational ability, virtues normally hidden in their segregated, shadow world.

Wearing a disguise to avoid Ras's revenge, the hero accidentally takes on the persona of the "renaissance man" of Harlem, Rinehart. The incredible Rinehart is a numbers runner, pimp, gang leader, police pay master, minister of the gospel, and, all round celebrity; his success illustrates the disordered individualism resulting from urban segregation. Rinehart, rind heart or heartless, offers a radical alternative to the leadership tradition of both Booker T. Washington and W.E.B. Du Bois. He represents the tyrannical self-enrichment possible through the ruthless exploitation of the Negro community by its "Talented Tenth." IM rejects Rinehartism, as he had earlier rejected the enforced political "liberation" of the Brotherhood, W.E.B. Du Bois's elitism, and Booker T. Washington's hopeful passivity. But the possibility of his "leadership" teaches IM about the trauma of the oppressed urban Blacks, as the riot provided him an insight into their virtues.

Visibility in Isolation

Freed from his last illusions about racial justice and liberation, IM now lives underground, totally free and "visible," but without social purpose. He resists oppression by fueling his subterranean vaults with pirated electricity from Monopolated Light and Power. His 1,369 (and growing) lights enable him to see himself. He is no longer invisible, as he had been when forced to see himself through the eyes of those, black and white, who denied him individuality. Having told his story in the novel, IM is a different man. He lives, as had his grandfather, in the light of the great principles of the Declaration of Independence—while acutely aware of the distance between principle and practice.

> Did he [his grandfather] mean "yes" because he knew that the principle was greater than the men, greater than the numbers and the vicious power and the methods used to corrupt its name? Did he mean to affirm the principle, which they themselves had brought into being out of the chaos and darkness of the feudal past, and which they had violated and compromised to the point of absurdity even in their own corrupt minds? Or did he mean that we had to take the responsibility for all of it, for the men as well as the principle, because we were the heirs who must use the principle because no other fitted our needs?

Living the Declaration's principles, he loves and hates his oppressors, who were also victims of racial stereotypes.

> And I defend (them) because in spite of all I find that I love. *In order to get some of it down I have to love.* I sell you no phony forgiveness, I'm a desperate man—but too much of your life will be lost, its meaning lost, unless you approach it as much through love as through hate. So I approach it through division. So I denounce and I defend and I hate and I love. (emphasis added)

Like *The Souls of Black Folk Invisible Man* ends pessimistically. Is the underground teacher of the evils of invisibility still a person? "I remind myself that the true darkness lies within my own mind, and the idea loses itself in gloom." ... IM still thinks "there's a possibility that even an invisible man has a socially responsible role to play." Yet, his isolation from the struggles, illusions, and passions of political life suggests that understanding, forgiveness, and even love, are insufficient bases for humanity.

Sexual Taboo in *Invisible Man*'s Battle Royal

Johnnie Wilcox

Johnnie Wilcox, a former assistant professor of English at Ohio University, specializes in postmodern American literature, critical theory, film, and new media.

In this essay, Wilcox examines the first chapter in Invisible Man, *which is often anthologized as the short story "Battle Royal." Wilcox explains that in the Battle Royal sequence, the white stripper provides a means through which the white men in attendance can sexualize their relationship to the black boys. The white men know that the naked white woman is the ultimate sexual taboo in the boys' world, and they use her, Wilcox argues, to empower themselves. The scene serves as a rite of passage for the narrator that reinforces the idea of white racial superiority and works to maintain white supremacy. The irony, however, Wilcox says, is that in the process of the woman's being held up as a taboo fetish, she becomes more linked with the black men than the white in the humiliation and dehumanization that they both suffer.*

Electricity is a substance, or medium, [in *Invisible Man*,] which conditions the narrator and other blacks for connection to larger systems of power and control, something the novel makes plain on several occasions, including (in order of occurrence) the Battle Royal, the Liberty Paints Factory Hospital, and the warm hole episodes. Like Tarp's leg-iron, the Battle Royal and the moments which lead to it can be read as metonyms of the generation of black labor and its conversion into forms useful to white-controlled systems of capital. Pub-

Johnnie Wilcox, "Black Power: Minstrelsy and Electricity in Ralph Ellison's Invisible Man," *Callalo*, v. 30, 2007. Copyright © 2007 by The Johns Hopkins University Press. Reproduced by permission of The Johns Hopkins University Press.

lished first as a short story, the Battle Royal episode is "a manufactured race riot and Dionysian orgy and coon show and circus entertainment and scapegoat sacrifice. It [is] an object lesson in humiliation, a sexual torture and castration rite [. . .]" Ellison has himself assented to one interviewer's similarly cast observation that "the Battle Royal as a false initiation rite (circumcision) is then really a castration rite." This ritualized castration happens at a smoker attended by "all of the town's big shots [who] were there in their tuxedoes, wolfing down the buffet foods, drinking beer and whiskey and smoking black cigars." These big shots simultaneously enact their power and prepare the narrator (and nine other young black men) for connection to a less visible but more pervasive system of production and control.

This preparation begins with a prelude wherein a "stark naked [. . .] magnificent blond" woman dances with "a slow sensuous movement; the smoke of a hundred cigars clinging to her like the thinnest of veils." First and foremost, the naked woman provides a means for the white men to sexualize their relationship to the black men. . . .

The dancing white woman with her naked body presents the young men with an icon of sexual desirability in a context where black male sexual desire is taboo. By staging the provocation of interracial sexual desire under their own watchful eyes, the white men position themselves both as censors and voyeurs. The narrator recalls, "She seemed like a fair bird-girl girdled in veils calling to me from the angry surface of some gray and threatening sea. I was transported. Then I became aware of the clarinet playing and the big shots yelling at us. Some threatened us if we looked and others if we did not." . . .

The suggestion is that the woman, like the black men, possesses double consciousness, that her subjective experience is antiparallel to the subjective experience of the young black men.

First, the blonde woman's "sensuous" movement anticipates the "infuriatingly sensuous motion" of the Sambo dolls
Tod Clifton hawks, both of which are forms of blackface minstrelsy. Furthermore, the blonde woman's distinguishing features span a racial and ethnic continuum: "the hair was yellow
like that of a circus kewpie doll, the face heavily powdered
and rouged, as though to form an abstract mask, the eyes hol-
low and smeared a cool blue, the color of a baboon's butt." In
what follows, the narrator specularly identifies with the naked
white woman through primitivist characteristics that signal
the woman's affinity with descendants of black Africans. . . .

The Point of Connection and Alienation

The naked woman is typed as an African primitive by means
of maskface while the veil theme is made explicit when she
begins dancing with "the smoke of a hundred cigars clinging
to her like the thinnest of veils." A further hint that she is a
minstrel figure comes in the smear of "cool blue" which suggests to the narrator a "baboon's butt," an animal native to
continental Africa and whose association with primitivism
and allusion to trickster identity are patent. However, in conflict with these intimations of the exotic, the woman is
branded as a domestic product by the "American flag tattooed
upon her belly," below which the narrator wishes to "stroke."
"Tattoo" is a homophone for her minstrelized dancing as well
as a reference to the subcutaneous ink branding her as a product "Made in the U.S.A."

The critical point of connection and alienation comes in
the narrator's imagined sense that he is the only object in her
visual field. The narrator specularly identifies with the naked
white woman, but this identification is undercut by the fact
that what he imagines to be an intimate and singular connection—"of all in the room she saw only me"—comes to him
through a set of "impersonal eyes." Despite her being in his
presence, her gaze is no more penetrating than the gaze of a
two-dimensional image, and the narrator's sense of signifi-

cance is equivalent to the feeling he might have while gazing into the eyes of a pin-up girl or an inanimate "kewpie doll."

Where the narrator does directly identify with the woman is in the domain of scopic agency. The woman's ocular reaction contradicts her facial reaction, and the narrator reads this separate visual signal as a sign of subjectival affinity. The narrator recounts that the drunken white men "caught her just as she reached the door, raised her from the floor, and tossed her as college boys are tossed at a hazing, and above her fixed-smiling lips I saw the terror and disgust in her eyes, almost like my own terror and that which I saw in some of the other boys." Here, the woman carries in her eyes a look of terror "almost like" the terror the narrator feels. There is an equivalence between the sexual fetishization of the woman as a blonde kewpie doll—an icon of sexual desirability and white supremacy—and the half-naked young black men about to box each other while blindfolded—symbols of sexual potency and neutralized threats to white male supremacy. The repression of black male sexual desire and the provocation of white female sexual disgust are part of the maintenance of an oppressive white male sexual power, a power predicated by the transformation of the white woman and the black men into objects of desire and objects of abjection. While the woman's dehumanization is complete once she has been transformed into a hypersexual automaton (a "circus kewpie doll"), the black men's sexualities are further channeled (transduced) into disorganized violence. The scene, then, traces an ideological pathway between black male desire for a white female sexual fetish and incoherent, black-on-black violence. The desiring apparatus of the black males is disconnected from the production of sexual desire and reconnected to human boxing machines.

A Disempowering Rite of Passage

The presence of this lone, hypersexualized female both disrupts and facilitates the exchange of power among all the men (white and black) at the smoker. In this prelude, the fetishiza-tion of sex under the sign of race forces a large, powerful, black man to "plead to go home" because his "dark red fight-ing trunks [are] much too small to conceal the erection which project[s] from him." At the same time, the racial and sexual imperatives structuring the relations between the parties present allows a drunken white man to sink his "beefy fingers" into the sexualized automaton's "soft flesh." Once she has been transformed into a sexual fetish, her presence reifies [makes real or concrete] the relationship between the white men as autonomous [self-governing, self-determining] agents and the black men as powerless thralls [people who are oppressed or enslaved]. As the narrator recalls, this differentiation is cata-lyzed by the blonde woman as she "continued dancing, smil-ing faintly at the big shots who watched her with fascination, and faintly smiling at our fear." The differential power rela-tions which obtain in the prelude confer prerogative and au-thority to the white male attendees, whatever their behavior. For example, one man "ran his hand through the thin hair of his bald head and, with his arms upheld, his posture clumsy like that of an intoxicated panda, wound his belly in a slow obscene grind." The white man's lewd dance is a degraded ver-sion of the naked blonde's tattoo and, like the blonde, his ra-cial identity is hybridized/ambiguous, represented by a panda whose fur is black and white. More to the point, this drunken white man can gesture obscenely with impunity because the presence of the white woman as sexual fetish legitimizes ev-erything he does, no matter what he does. By the same racial logic, the young black men must conceal even the involuntary erections they experience when forced to watch the woman's "slow sensuous movement."

The woman's presence as a racial and sexual fetish anneals [strengthens] the inconsistencies of the prelude's racial-desiring, her whiteness sanctioning the desire and actions of the white men and outlawing the desire and reactions of the black men. Racial-desiring here produces three racial formations: the empowered white men, the disempowered black men, and an icon of white female sexuality that is catalyst and object of the ensemble's racial-desiring. Ellison has said that the Battle Royal "was a rite which could be used to project certain racial divisions into the society and reinforce the idea of white racial superiority."

Maintaining White Supremacy

As catalyst, the woman facilitates the production of racial formations and the transmission of white supremacist ideology in a more or less orderly fashion, but her presence also inspires some of the white men to transgress the unspoken prohibition against touching. When this happens, the ensemble stops functioning smoothly. It stutters, further differentiating the white men into those who behave like "intoxicated panda[s]" and those who assist the woman in her escape. The differing spontaneous reactions of these men suggests that sexuality, like race, generates contradictory responses even from subjects located inside the system. In other words, the woman as sexual fetish is an ideological object that stitches [together] the inconsistencies of the several racial-sexual subject positions which come into being by the fact of her very presence. She is a rent in the racial-desiring of this prelude to black-on-black violence, a gap that introduces a margin of indetermination into the prelude's closed circuit of sexual desire and racial oppression. She is both the defiler and the defilement, and she makes the racial-sexual relationship between the white men and the black men work.

Taken as an allegory of the preparation of black males for the system of American capital, the prelude to the Battle Royal trains these young black men-about-to-become-machines to disavow their organismic impulses when in the presence of a white sexual fetish. The young black men are taught how to read a symbol of white female sexuality. Ellison believed that "anyone writing from the Negro American point of view would certainly have had to write about the potential meaning and the effects of the relationship between [. . .] black men and white women, because [. . .] a great part of [American] society was controlled by the taboos built around the fear of the white woman and the black man getting together." The prelude to the Battle Royal illustrates the way in which (1930s-era) American racial-desiring produces white supremacy as a mechanism that prohibits the consummation of black male sexual desire for a fetishized white woman, a process that ironically links the white woman with the black men even as it dehumanizes them.

Ellison's Liberty Paints Represents Racist America

Randy Boyagoda

Randy Boyagoda is a writer, critic, and scholar who has contributed to publications such as Harper's *and the* New York Times. *He is an associate professor of American studies in the English Department at Ryerson University in Toronto.*

In the following viewpoint Boyagoda explains Ellison's hostility toward immigrants during the 1930s and 1940s. Ellison resented that immigrants benefited from America's racially divided social system by passing into the white population. Boyagoda argues that in Invisible Man, *Ellison creates a stigmatized version of immigrants. Immigrant difference is highly visible in the novel, serving as a catalyst for the protagonist to assert his own American identity by comparison. In the Liberty Paints section of the novel, especially, the narrator finds himself in conflict with new immigrants and southern blacks. The company, Boyagoda says, represents black and white America. The narrator's employment there sparks competing expressions of identity among those who favor union solidarity or national solidarity.*

The presence of immigrants in 1930s and 1940s New York City complicated Ralph Ellison's ambitions for black Americans and provoked in him a persistent hostility towards their competing claims for recognition as fellow citizens. During a 1977 writers' discussion, for example, Ellison's response to a leading question from Ishmael Reed about immigrant attitudes towards the United States reveals an unmistakably sour position. It is tacitly but firmly based upon his view of a fundamental disjunction between responsibility for past wrongs and reception of present promise:

Randy Boyagoda, *Race, Immigration, and American Identity in the Fiction of Salman Rushdie, Ralph Ellison, and William Faulkner.* Routledge, 2008. Copyright © 2008 by Taylor & Francis Group LCC—Books. Reproduced with permission of Taylor & Francis Group LCC—Books via Copyright Clearance Center.

Some simply feel nostalgic for the certainties of the societies they left behind. I don't think that most of them bring their disdain with them. They develop it after discovering the difference between the American dream and our day-to-day American reality; a complex reality which is consistently questioned by our condition and our protests. On the other hand, that kind of disdain is a put-down which an immigrant might well find irresistible. They didn't create the negative aspect of our society; they weren't here, and most would deny that they even benefited from the injustices we've had to live with—although they damn well have, and do.

Ellison complains that the problem with immigrant passages into American society is that not only do they exempt themselves from responsibility for past injustices (such as slavery), they also benefit from America's race-divided social system by easily passing into the white population [since most were European].

Elsewhere, he explicitly cites the presence of immigrants as impeding modern America's acceptance of its native blacks as nationally equal to their white counterparts. In the ominously entitled essay "What America Would Be Like Without Blacks" (1970), Ellison explains one reason for perpetual black exclusion and archly notes those responsible for it:

Many whites could look at the social position of blacks and feel that color formed an easy and reliable gauge for determining to what extent one was or was not American. Perhaps that is why one of the first epithets that many European immigrants learned when they got off the boat was "nigger"; it made them feel instantly American.

While blacks have suffered through two centuries of degradation, and yet maintain their allegiance to a nation that refuses to grant them full status as fellow citizens, white immigrants feel "instantly" American based upon their easy entry into America's pre-existing racial hierarchies. This frustration leads

Ellison to argue in turn that a full understanding of U.S. national identity depends upon one indisputable fact: "the troubling suspicion that whatever else the *true* American is, he is also somehow black" (emphasis mine).

Ellison Stigmatizes Immigrants

In *Invisible Man*, Ellison establishes this version of an indigenous American identity by positioning it against nationally defined outsiders. He was provoked into this strategy by the challenges that newly arrived immigrants posed to his locally circumscribed conceptions of national community and American identity. The strategies that Invisible Man deploys in combating foreigners in New York reveal why, how, and when local communities depend upon what [anthropologist Arjun] Appadurai explains as a primordialist concept of collective identity. Primordialists reject common connections uprooted from specific, continuously homogenous locales; instead, they endorse "attachments that bind small, intimate collectivities . . . based upon shared claims to blood, soil, [and] language." In response to what he saw as the persistent non-recognition of black contributions to America's composition and culture, Ellison uses *Invisible Man* to enact the "self-expression" and support the "cultural survival" that constitute the positive form of a "culturalist" mobilization of group identity. This gambit, however, involves a strong, if thus far understudied, xenophobic element. Immigrants are stigmatized in *Invisible Man* by their intertwined associations with languages and political interests deemed un-American when measured against the commitments and culture of southern blacks. What I call invisible immigrants act as catalytic elements in the novel; their foreignness comes into high visibility so that the protagonist can assert his primordial American identity—as an ambivalent but self-affirmed black southerner—as justification for being recognized as American by comparison with suspicious, dangerous immigrants.

[Author] Glenn Loury has noted that blacks migrating to the North in the first half of the twentieth century met with "fierce resistance from the relatively new Americans of that day." This was a further burden for "these sons and daughters of slaves," which, according to Loury, could only be corrected through a universal recognition of "the equal humanity" of all Americans. Ellison would readily agree with this humanist approach to race relations and determining national identity, and he would likely agree with the immigrant challenge that members of the Great Migration had to confront. In his writing, he sought to resist the fragmentation of modern life brought about by (the Great) migration and communal dissolution; through *Invisible Man*, he tests organic national identity, defined by a cultural reformulation of black America's historical and racial scars, as an answer to the disintegrations of native black community in modern America. He sends the novel's protagonist off in search of continuity between his southern past and northern present, his rural roots and urban consciousness. In so committing his only major fiction to such a task, Ellison joined a history of writing on black aspirations for national recognition complicated by immigrant competition, including work by Alain Locke and the contributors to *The New Negro* [a 1925 anthology edited by Locke], and by Booker T. Washington.

Being Both "Negro and American"

Ellison's formula for American identity most directly resembles [early twentieth-century black intellectual] W.E.B. DuBois's, as put forth in *The Souls of Black Folk* (1903). Early in that work, after famously lamenting the native black's "two-ness—an American, a Negro," DuBois calls for a merging of these "warring ideals" through a middle way between the monolithic options then available:

> [The American Negro] would not Africanize America, for America has too much to teach the world and Africa. He

would not bleach his Negro soul in a flood of white Americanism, for he knows that the Negro has a message for the world. He simply wishes to make it possible for a man to be both a Negro and an American, without being cursed and spit upon by his fellows, without having the doors of Opportunity closed roughly in his face.

In *Invisible Man*, Ellison evokes the opposed extremities of expatriation and self-erasure that DuBois describes, and rejects both paths. Instead, the novel endorses the internally hybrid identity that *Souls* also holds up—to be both "Negro and American" and thus "a co-worker in the [national] culture." In committing to such a goal, Ellison—long considered strongly conservative—was in fact more heterodox [unorthodox] than he initially seemed, contends [literary critic] Henry Louis Gates, Jr.: "[For Ellison,] the revolutionary political act was not separation; it was the staking of a claim for the Negro in the construction of an honestly public American culture." Rather than rejecting a nation that had historically rejected his race, Ellison sought to establish, through historically defined experiences and cultural expressions, the very Americanness of native blacks. Yet in staking this claim while trying to avoid the "door of Opportunity closed roughly in his face," Ellison's protagonist has to contend with elements that exist outside of the binaries [dualities] that he, like DuBois's famous seventh son, so valued. Before both DuBois and Ellison, Booker T. Washington registered a similar commitment to black national identity, though he sensed it was challenged by changes to America's population. . . .

Liberty Paints: Keeping America Pure

Invisible Man's blindly optimistic ambitions manage to persist beyond his early, unsettling encounter with Ras, and beyond homesickness, repeated employment rejections, and revelations about Bledsoe's letters of recommendation. In finally finding work at Liberty Paints, however, the character loses

A family of immigrants at New York's Ellis Island in the 1930s. © FPG/Staff/Getty Images.

whatever hopefulness still lingers, finding himself in a position that remains his for the rest of the novel: caught between new immigrants and southern blacks, pulled towards and pushed away by both while confronted by a strategically color-blind nation. He is greeted with a loaded slogan on his first day of work: "KEEP AMERICA PURE WITH LIBERTY PAINTS." His first duty suggests the seeming impossibility of achieving this famous purity: he is told to add drops of black liquid to white paint and mix them together. [Literary critic] Kerry Mc-Sweeney suggests that Ellison "hints at a whitewash designed to absorb black Americans into a sanitized history of American life—to cover the black truth with a glossy white mythology." This reading pays inadequate attention to the metaphorical underpinnings of the whitening process. The whiteness of this paint requires a component of blackness to achieve its purity; the color represents not so much the disappearance of black Americans into a purely white national myth as the dependence of that myth on the inclusion of blackness. The painting allegory is indeed a critique of black complicity in the ongoing whitewash of national history, but is also the revelation of blackness as a constituent element of American identity.

Ellison expands this allegory by sending his protagonist underground to Liberty Paints' boiler room, where, to Invisible Man's confused presumption that "'the paint was made upstairs,'" the crotchety Brockway replies:

> "Naw, they just mixes in the color, make it look pretty. Right down here is where the real paint is made. Without what I do they couldn't do nothing, they be making bricks without straw . . . caint a single doggone drop of paint move out of the factory lessen it comes through Lucius Brockway's hands."

North and South, White and Black

If Liberty Paints allegorically "represents America," then the national image is prettied above but forged below, white on the surface but black beneath. Brockway is slavishly devoted to Old Man Sparland and, given the calamities that befall Liberty's white paints when Lucas is temporarily absent, proves himself indispensable to the operation. Two important geographical elements here emerge. While we are never told explicitly that he is a southerner, it seems reasonable to assume—based upon his age, his attitude towards white authority, and his southern-inflected language—that Brockway is an early member of the Great Migration. In terms of spatial symbolism, the distinctions he makes about the factory, between below and above, suggests a North/South division. The white national image of America is borne by the black South in its migration to northern factories and in its historically servile relation to the nation at large. Ellison represents both of these black contributions to the wider nation as tactically effaced, with blacks complicit in the denial.

A throwaway comment confirms this wider possibility for Ellison's paint-factory-as-national-allegory. After proudly informing his would-be apprentice that he came up with the slogan for the company's most popular paint, Brockway again boasts of his indispensability: "'Ain't a *continental* thing that happens down here ain't as iffen I done put my *black* hands into it!'" (emphases mine). Ellison's choice of adjective holds geographic implications; most every action—continent-wide—that ensures white success has a black component. Unmoved by Brockway's self-aggrandizement, [writer Gregory] Stephens regards the character as symbolizing the "complicity of blacks in this act [of whitewashing America], and [in the] conditions of underpaid and under-recognized servitude under which blacks perform their role." Indeed, the character seems willing to fulfill one of the negative options that DuBois lays out in *Souls*: the black man willing to "bleach his Negro soul in a flood of white Americanism." As we shall see, however, the regional dimension of Brockway's black pride in white paint renders it, at the very least, indicative of an inherently national, historically based problem that Invisible Man will struggle to modify and correct. When he innocuously goes off in search of his lunch, Invisible Man encounters an unexpected, newer difficulty facing Great Migration blacks in New York.

Troublemaking Immigrants

In seeking success in the North, an ambition symbolized by his moving upstairs from the southern setting of Brockway's boiler room, Invisible Man stumbles into a meeting of factory workers. Informing an interlocutor that Lucius Brockway is his foreman, he receives an unexpectedly harsh response. "'Get him the hell out of here,' they shouted. I turned. A group on the far side of the room kicked over a bench, yelling, 'Throw him out! Throw him out!'" The angry words echo the "'We gine chase 'em out!'" refrain that welcomed Invisible Man to Harlem, though the deeper parallel between the respective speakers is not initially clear. The workers at Liberty Paints are organizing into a union; their rationale for rejecting Invisible Man involves a racial prejudice that becomes evident as their deliberations intensify. One union man's seeming sympathy is based upon the presumption of certain differences between those who work above and those who work below. His offending benevolence anticipates Ellison's sarcastic depictions of the well-meaning white activists of the Brotherhood: "'we don't want to forget that workers like him aren't so highly developed as some of us who've been in the labor movement for a long time.'" The put-down ostensibly occurs along an experiential divide, though the protagonist senses a racial tone to the euphemistic "workers like him" and "some of us" distinctions. When he returns downstairs, however, this rather simple black-white split is reformulated along more complex national lines, through fanatical appeals to racial and regional solidarity.

Invisible Man receives yet another loud and unexpected rejection, this time from Brockway, when he mentions the union meeting: "*Union!* I heard his white cup shatter against the floor as he uncrossed his legs, rising. 'I knowed you belonged to that bunch of troublemaking foreigners! I knowed it! Git out!' he screamed. 'Git out of my basement!'" Another exclamatory dismissal leaves Invisible Man feeling roundly rejected. Earlier, he was confronted with foreign-accented, divisive sentiments that framed his arrival in Harlem; now, he is rejected by the union for his apparent association with Brockway, and rejected by Brockway for his apparent association with the union. Brockway despises the union for its foreignness, which, in a historical context, relates to its predominantly immigrant composition. [Historian] David Reimers explains that Eastern European immigrants to New York "became active in the city's growing trade unions" between 1880 and [World War II], while [historian] Seth Scheiner observes that "those southern Negroes who migrated northward brought with them the southern antipathy for unions." In response to the interconnection of unions and immigrants, Brockway projects a fantastic vision of rosy plantation life onto a northern factory and regards union membership as a betrayal of one's race, one's nation, and of idealized, benevolent black-white relations in America: "'That damn union,' he cried, almost in tears. 'That *damn* union! They after my job! I knew they after my job! For one of us to join one of them damned unions is like we was to bite the hand of the man who teached us how to bathe in a bathtub!'"

The Destabilizing Third Element

Brockway's response registers the anxiety of the native-born forced to contend for his well-being with an outside challenge. Against this newness, anything rooted and historically based—even an idealized vision of updated plantation relations—is acceptable because it is knowable within the parameters of a continuous, stable, and indigenous narrative. [Critic] Richard Kostelanetz regards this chapter of *Invisible Man* "as a symbolic portrait of the underlying reality of black-white relations in America," through which Ellison reveals "the heretical truth that American life, underneath the white surface, is like the color grey, indeed a mixture of black and white." This observation, while attentive to the chapter's blurring of neat racial distinctions, does not account for how (native) black and white in fact harmonize, at least for Brockway. He regards the presence of union men as a destabilizing third element outside indigenous black/white relations; these troublemaking immigrants are intent upon taking black jobs and will break apart traditional American race relations, in turn demanding unity on the native side that denies all internal problems in the face of outsiders.

Invisible Man inimically views the old man as beholden to an understanding of black-white relations that holds in contemporary New York only through zealous denials of foreign otherness and fantasy images of black-white, master-slave relations. But while Invisible Man finds problems with Brockway's regionalist limitations, he is similarly dissatisfied with the union's offerings. Moreover, he becomes the unwitting catalyst for competing expressions of identity—union solidarity based upon tacitly racial and immigrant unity vs. national solidarity supported by racial regional connections. His consequent position, a version of the "tight spot" motif that [critic] Houston Baker discerns in the novel, recurs throughout *Invisible Man*: he is stuck between sectarian foreigners and lame black southerners—uneasy, alienated, and intent upon a new option.

Ellison, Memory, and the Act of Writing in *Invisible Man*

W. James Booth

W. James Booth is a professor in the Political Science and Philosophy Departments at Vanderbilt University in Nashville, Tennessee. He is the author of Communities of Memory: On Witness, Identity, and Justice.

In the following viewpoint, Booth argues that memory and the act of writing are essential components of Invisible Man. *Memories of America's troublesome discriminatory past haunt the characters in the novel and have a continuing impact on justice and identity. Booth contends that Ellison concerns himself with an enduring presence of the past and the everydayness of race. He writes in a vernacular language in* Invisible Man *to capture the locales of the African American past. In Ellison's work, Booth asserts, both the past and the future lurk and interact with one another, as do memory and hope, and race and American democratic life.*

In this essay, I am concerned with the relationship between the visibility of race as color, the memory of injustice, and American identity. The visibility of color would seem to make it a daily reminder of race and its history, and in this way to be intimately a part of American memory and identity. Yet the tie between memory and color is anything but certain or transparent. Rather, as I shall argue, it is a latticework composed of things remembered, forgotten, glossed, or idealized, and the traces they leave in our world, traces that keep that past from falling into the oblivion of forgetfulness. Finally, color, memory, and identity together belong to the struggle

W. James Booth, "The Color of Memory: Reading Race with Ralph Ellison," *Political Theory*, v. 36, October, 2008. Copyright © 2008 by SAGE Publication. All rights reserved. Reproduced by permission of SAGE Publications, Inc.

over racial justice in this country, a battle in part to recognize the past, of which color is the visible reminder.

Ralph Ellison's writings, and particularly his defining work, the *Invisible Man*, map these issues and some of the ways of approaching them. The present essay is an exploration of those questions, conducted through an engagement with his work. The *Invisible Man* speaks to race, justice, and memory, but obliquely, refracted through the vernacular. Ellison's use of the vernacular, the "lower frequencies" of race, creates special challenges (and opportunities) for the political theorist: challenges because we are perhaps accustomed to a more clearly delineated political domain, evident for example in laws, court cases, constitutions, legislatures, parties, and so on. The indirectness of the *Invisible Man* thus gives rise to the question, "Where are the politics?" And it offers opportunities, as for example in Ellison's suggestion that an important dimension of politics is to be found outside of the domain of high civics and in the vernacular, in how citizens live together, speak to one another, in what they remember and forget, in what they hope for, or in a future they ignore or reject. From that oblique vantage point is to be seen part of his contribution to our understanding of race in America. . . .

Allow me to start with some thematic remarks on reading the *Invisible Man*. The story begins with this epigraph, a passage from Herman Melville's "Benito Cereno:" "'You are saved,' cried Captain Delano, more and more astonished and pained: 'you are saved: what has cast such a shadow upon you?'" To be saved, yet still to be darkened as if by a shadow. In Melville's novel, Delano, an American, makes this remark urging Benito to forget the past, just (he says) as the sun, sea, and sky "have turned over new leaves." Benito answers that the sea and sky "have no memory . . . because they are not human." The shadow here is cast by the memory of a slave revolt on his ship, or perhaps by slavery itself. Delano's (characteristically American) appeal to turn away from the past expresses an optimism, and a future-directed gaze, made possible, in part, by forgetting. Ellison, too, wrote of shadows, and in particular "the shadow of [the] past." His choice of these lines from Melville suggests that central to Ellison's understanding of race and justice in America is memory as a vehicle of the presence of the past, the shadows it casts, the resulting temptation to forget, and the relationship of past and future.

The Shadows of the Past

"To be saved:" the Civil War, the Emancipation Proclamation, the Civil Rights struggle, the ending of legalized segregation, and so on all had brought African Americans more fully into their country's political and economic life. Yet, and at the same time, race and its history here remain a powerful and troubling presence, whether in the lingering and observable effects of past discriminatory policies, in ongoing debates over affirmative action, diversity, and reparations, or in their myriad daily forms. Theirs is surely also a haunting presence, the memory of past injustice. The shadows of those centuries continue to fall upon America, however much the institutionalized landscape of race relations may have changed, and however much, like Delano, some might wish to turn over a new leaf. America, on this reading, is caught between, on the one side, the enduring presence of the past and, on the other side, the belief or hope that a non-racial society is near, between a kind of memorylessness and sunny optimism and the sense that the past has not yet been mastered, or even fully addressed. Perhaps Ellison's thought in choosing that Melville passage was that America is both Delano and Cerano, the will to forget, the orientation to the future, and the intrusive presence of the past in memory, and their impact on identity and justice.

For Ellison, memory was central. "The act of writing," he said, "requires a constant plunging back into the shadow of the past where time hovers ghostlike." In the *Invisible Man*, that maxim guides both the account of the particularity of the

African American experience and the universal ambitions of the novel. Here I want to unfold and refine that claim through these three more detailed observations. First, Ellison was sharply critical of what he took to be an oversimplifying emphasis on race, and a neglect of the "complex resources" of the African American heritage including its part in a shared American experience. He is therefore often read, and sometimes criticized or praised, as an author who resisted the idea of race and culture, offering in its place a view of (or hope for) the United States as post-racial, though fed from the tributaries of its many communities. To be sure, Ellison objected to a narrow focus on race, and to the idea of a black culture apart from its context, preferring instead to emphasize its diversity and its place in the confluence of American life. By the same token, America (its past, its identity, its remembering, and amnesia) was not one unitary thing. Rather, America in his view was formed by the interweaving of its constituent communities, communities that share a history of conflict and injustice and contribute their voices to its culture without losing their distinctive paths on that common journey. So, too, what is remembered and forgotten belong to that American quilt work, present in different ways across its breadth. When, with Ellison, I use terms such as American identity, optimism, memory, or amnesia, it is in the sense just outlined: compound and shifting rather than unitary and stable. His is not an essentialist understanding of that experience, but rather rests on the thought that it belongs to a community of memory with a past of injustice, a heritage, and the culture it informs, and with color as a reminder of that particularity.

The Everydayness of Race

Second, Ellison is also sometimes read (and criticized) as an author either lost in a bittersweet nostalgia for the past of his Oklahoma youth, or in a dreamy commitment to the future post-racial America of his hopes rather than to its far less attractive present. Ellison did refer to his "pioneer background" and to Oklahoma, the "young state" and the "territory of his dreams," as [literary scholar] Lawrence Jackson calls it. In that same interview, though, Ellison recalled that his mother had been raised on a Georgia plantation, and that this family history had given him a more complete "sense of the past." In an earlier (1965) interview, he was confronted with this pointed critique, suggesting a too rosy future-oriented optimism: "you are expressing your own hopes and aspirations for Negroes, rather than reporting historical reality." He responded that "hope and aspiration are indeed important aspects of the reality of Negro American history." Hope and waiting, however, were always wedded to the fact that African American "consciousness . . . is a product of our memory" and not of "a will to historical forgetfulness." American optimism, on the other hand, rested in no small part on just such a forgetting, a making invisible, of its own past. "We don't remember enough; we don't allow ourselves to remember events, and I suppose this helps us to continue our belief in progress." Ellison wrote not with nostalgia or optimism but with a concern for the enduring presence of the African American past, and thus for the place of memory in identity and in justice. Justice called for a dealing with the past, but it also tempered that retrospective glance by binding it to "hope and aspiration," to what Ellison termed a "watchful waiting." Memory work, then, was not a bitter reliving of the past but rather an insistence on its continued presence, transformed by present invention and always potentially emancipatory: "This is the use of memory: for liberation . . . From the future as well as the past . . . See, now they vanish, The faces and places, with the self which, as it could, loved them, to become renewed, transfigured, in another pattern."

Third, Ellison explored the ties between color, memory, and identity in their everyday forms, their "lower frequencies," and he came to understand them as richly as he did precisely because he attended to their place in the daily currency of life in America. In thinking about identity, memory, and race as they are given in that everydayness, Ellison draws us into meanings of these phenomena that can easily be lost sight of when they become, as they sometimes do in the scholarly literature, placeholders for an array of theoretical concerns and policy issues. He was scornful of what he termed the "burden of sociology," which tended, he thought, to subordinate the diversity of African American life to a "metaphysical condition." The turn to the vernacular was, however, more than a rejection of the academic's monochromatic abstractions as it was also more than the literary cultivation of a popular style. The vernacular, he said, was the dynamic process and interaction of the past and of present invention. It was the "stream of history" for a people denied a place in their country's civic history. It contains the "reminders of the past as Negroes recalled it . . . [and] passed [it] along . . ." The many forms of the vernacular are the locales of the African American past. Yet as the passage above suggests, that act of finding also involved a dynamic interplay of past recovered and present invention, and of remembrance and a watchful hope for the future. The familiar and the past were, for him, midwife to the new.

Relationship of Past, Present, and Future

In sum, Ellison was concerned with the everydayness of race in America, its vernacular inflected by the past and the future, by memory and the hopeful waiting for justice. It belongs to the subtlety of Ellison's writing that he leads his readers to see the relationship between the weight of the unchosen past made available in memory and the future with its characteristic indeterminacy and openness. This is apparent already in the locale in which the *Invisible Man* is set: a bustling, multiracial tableau, in a word, a place where the future or at least an intimation of it casts its shadow, too. There both the past and the future lurk and interact, neither entirely visible, the one "around the corner," the other the subject of a "watchful waiting." There, too, the vernacular, the stability and fixity of color/race rooted in memory, are in part disrupted or made ambiguous. In the preacher's words early on in the *Invisible Man*: "I said black is . . . an' black ain't . . ." One does not triumph over the other. The weight of the past is not lifted but nor does the shadow it casts overwhelm the watchful waiting for the future. Rather, memory and hope, past and future, race and American democratic life are all to be seen there, and together they mark out the horizon of Ellison's work. Yet within that complex horizon, the focus on memory in this essay is, I would suggest, appropriate and consistent with Ellison's argument. He thought that, in the end, the core American failing was a flight from the burdens of its own past, and he wanted to bring that deep flaw into the light of day even while pointing to its manifold interaction with the present and future.

Social Issues
in Literature

Contemporary
Perspectives on Race

It Is Time to Stop Using the Word *Minority* for All Nonwhites

Barry Cross Jr.

Barry Cross Jr. is the president and chairman of Elsie Y. Cross Associates, a group that partners with client organizations to institute comprehensive and strategic change that ensures the integration of all marginalized groups into the workforce. He is also the publisher of the quarterly online journal Diversity Factor.

In the following essay, Cross encourages readers to stop using the word minority *to refer to all nonwhite people. He believes that the term does not distinguish between the multiple textures of culture, ethnicity, and race. Instead, it lumps groups with very different values, customs, and cultures together. Furthermore, Cross argues that the use of* minority *creates an Us and Them mentality and is disrespectful to all nonwhites. He suggests that a more appropriate term for groups of people whose ethnicity, nationality, or race is not immediately known is* people of color.

Following Sonia Sotomayor's [2009] nomination to the Supreme Court, I have gotten more concerned and frustrated with how the media and conservative pundits are using the term "minority." The word has become code for everyone who is not a White male. The use of the term prevents us from noticing diversity's differences and having an open and honest discussion about the benefits of diversity. We should be talking about why it is valid, useful and important to have different points of view based on social identity in the Supreme Court and in society in general.

Barry Cross Jr., "Publisher's Perspective: Isn't It Time To Stop Using the Term 'Minority' to Describe All Individuals, Racial and Ethnic Groups Who are Not White?," *The Diversity Factor*, v. 17, Spring, 2009. Reproduced by permission.

It is my strong belief that the courts should reflect the demographics of our nation's population and not just the experience of one group. It is not that I think any one group is better or more qualified than another. I value representative— that is, inclusive—government of the people, by the people, and for the people.

An example of one of those frustrating and confusing comments on this topic came from Huma Khan and Jake Tapper of ABC News, who were quoted as saying: "Conservative pundit Ann Coulter said on *Good Morning America*, 'Saying that someone who would decide a case differently . . . because she's a Latina, not a white male,' that statement by definition is racist. It does a disservice to minorities—to women and minorities.'"

First, the most remarkable aspect of that statement is Ann Coulter's denial that her own experience as a White woman plays any part in her thinking and judgment. Secondly, her use of the word "minorities" is condescending. I prefer to use the term "People of Color" over the term "minorities" when I describe racial and ethnic groups who are not White. The term "People of Color" is neutral, and does not have the negative implications as the term "minorities," which seems to imply something "less than" being White.

Unexpressive of the Texture of Culture

Using the term "minority," and even Hispanic, paints a picture with too broad a brush. This terminology does not distinguish the textures of culture, ethnicity and race, nor does it notice or attempt to understand different experiences, realities and perspectives by social group identity. For example, if we use the term "minority" to describe everyone who is not White, we miss the differences between Arabs, Asians, Blacks, Hispanics, and Native Americans. These are very different groups

On August 8, 2009, Justice Sonia Sotomayor, who is Puerto Rican, became the first person of Hispanic descent to serve on the Supreme Court. © The White House/Handout/Getty Images.

with different values, customs and cultures. Similarly, simply using the term "Hispanic" to describe Sonia Sotomayor is misleading because it doesn't identify her as a Puerto Rican.

By saying that Sotomayor is Puerto Rican, we would know that she is a Latina born as a U.S. citizen whose official language is Spanish. We might also surmise that due to her Puerto Rican heritage, her views on immigration and other issues could be very different from the views of other Hispanics such as Cubans, Mexicans or Venezuelans.

My view of the term "minorities" is reflected in the definition of minorities found on Wikipedia [as of June 5, 2009]:

> A "minority" is a sociological group that does not constitute a politically dominant voting majority of the total population of a given society. A sociological "minority" is not necessarily a numerical "minority". It may include any group that is subnormal with respect to a dominant group in terms of social status, education, employment, wealth, and political power. In socioeconomics, the term "minority" typically refers to a socially subordinate ethnic group (understood in terms of color, language, nationality, religion, sexual orientation, and/or culture). Other groups called "minorities" include people with disabilities, "economic minorities" (working poor or unemployed), "age minorities" (who are younger or older than a typical working age) and people with different sexual orientations.

An "Us and Them" Mentality

So no wonder I am offended when I am called a "minority," and it surprises me that others are unaware. Personally, I consider myself Black or sometimes I may identify myself as an African-American. But I do not see myself as a "minority"—someone who is "less than" someone who is in the "majority." It is even more surprising and disappointing to me when I see the liberal or progressive media outlets and even President [Barack] Obama use the term "minority" to describe individuals or groups of people. I am even more puzzled when I see diversity publications using the term "minority" instead of "People of Color" or the actual racial or ethnic group to which they are referring.

This is not about being politically correct. This is about respecting people for who they are and making an effort to acknowledge their heritage, ethnicity, culture, race, and/or experience. Calling everyone who is non-White a "minority" is disrespectful and lazy. Think about it, we don't call White people the "majority." Most White people don't consider themselves a group, however; they experience others as "minority" groups.

The more appropriate way to describe someone or a group when you don't know their ethnicity, nationality, or race would be as a Person of Color for individuals or People of Color at the group level or for mixed groups. However, if you do know their heritage, it is always best to use that. I would say the same is true for the terms Hispanic and Asian. Both terms cover a wide range of cultures and nationalities. So again, if you do not know that person's ethnicity then it would [be] more appropriate to be curious and ask what race or ethnicity best represents the person you are describing. Accept how they self-identify.

While the term "minority" is commonly used by the media, human rights groups and in various government documents and policies, it subordinates groups, places a negative label on people and racializes the term. Let's move away from creating an "us and them" two-group mentality and get to know who we really are by our social group identity and see, acknowledge, and accept our differences and similarities. Reducing everyone who is not White to a "minority" continues to make individuals and groups invisible.

Color Blindness Suggests People Are Embarrassed to Talk About Race

Sam Sommers

Sam Sommers is a social psychologist at Tufts University in Medford, Massachusetts. He is also a blogger for Psychology Today.

In this article, Sommers argues that when people try to avoid recognizing race by cultivating color blindness, it does nothing to foster relationships between different cultures. In fact, Sommers claims, color blindness simply suggests that people either do not know how to talk about race or they are embarrassed to do so. Some people feel that if they admit that they notice someone's skin color they might be considered racist, but Sommers says this is not so. It is perfectly natural to notice racial differences among people. The problem, Sommers argues, is that the older people get, the less likely they are to talk openly about these differences. Sommers contends that race should not be an embarrassment. He hopes parents will teach their children to embrace racial differences so that they will be open to recognizing and discussing difference in all walks of life.

A Mother checks out the produce while her 3-year-old happily jabbers away from his perch at the front of their grocery cart. In the midst of an exuberant soliloquy lengthy enough to make [William] Shakespeare or [Vice President] Joe Biden proud, the young boy suddenly points to a fellow shopper and exclaims, "Mommy, look—that man has a brown face!"

How will Mommy respond? By smiling? Perhaps with, Why, yes, he does, and you have a pink one? Or maybe, That's true, but pointing isn't polite, so how about waving hello instead?

At my local grocery store, the answer is none of the above.

When I recently encountered this scenario, Mommy's response was one of sheer terror. It was the shade of her face that was most interesting—she was I-Just-Saw-A-Ghost Pale in crayon parlance. She couldn't even muster a verbal reply, and instead sped away like a bank robber.

American society is increasingly one in which people (especially white people) embrace the idea of color blindness. Mind you, I'm not talking about the dream articulated by [civil rights leader] Martin Luther King decades ago, that one day his children would be judged by their characters instead of their color. No, I'm talking about a dream that's been embraced by Stephen Colbert's mocking persona [on Comedy Central's *The Daily Show*]: the effort to appear literally color-blind by claiming not to notice race.

Noticing Race Does Not Make One Racist

We often hesitate to use race as a descriptor: Maybe you can recall a friend saying something like, "He's about my height, mid-30s, dresses well . . ." and then, only after looking around nervously to see who was listening, "and he's . . . black . . ."

Consider the observations of Janet Schofield, a psychologist who once assessed a junior high school in which the teachers, by administrative decree, avoided any mention of race in the classroom. She reported the amazing story that some students were surprised to learn during an interview with the researchers that Dr. King was a black man.

In research with my colleagues at Tufts and Harvard, we've found that the underlying motivation is the thought that if I don't notice race, then I definitely can't be called a racist.

Americans think that feigning color blindness is the safest way to handle a potentially dicey topic.

You can see this mentality in the tendency of many white Americans to prefer a root canal to any discussion of race. You can see it in the knee-jerk dismissal called "playing the race card" levied against anyone who dares talk about racial issues. You can see it in the parent who reacts to her child's mention of race as if it were an epithet or insult. After a while, kids pick up on this message.

In one study we asked elementary school students to play a variation on the game Guess Who, in which they had to ask yes-or-no questions to figure out which photo, from a set, their partner was holding.

The children were given a set of photos of white faces that varied on a number of dimensions, including age, weight, facial expression, and background color. It took 10- and 11-year-olds fewer questions to identify the target than 8- and 9-year-olds. No surprise there: As they get older, kids get better at categorization, problem solving, and logical reasoning.

But an interesting thing happened when we threw race into the mix. When half the photos were of white faces and half of black faces, the performance advantage of the older kids disappeared. In fact, it reversed: Suddenly it was the younger kids who were quicker to get the right answer.

Why the change? Because the older kids wouldn't ask about race. While 77 percent of the younger children talked about skin color, only 37 percent of the older children did. In other words, at a young age, kids start to master the skill of categorizing people on dimensions like gender, race, age, and attractiveness. (This tendency seems to be at least somewhat innate; even infants perceptually differentiate between racial groups.) And then, a few years down the road, they learn that they're only supposed to admit to using some of these social categories.

Should Skin Color Be Embarrassing?

Should we care that increasing numbers of Americans are claiming to be color-blind, even though neuroscientific data reveal that we notice race within 150 milliseconds of meeting someone?

Actually, yes. Our research suggests that you typically don't make the good impression you might think you will by going out of your way to avoid acknowledging race. When we show people silent video clips of adult participants trying to complete a photo description task without talking about race, such "color-blind" individuals are rated as distracted, interpersonally cold and distant, and disingenuous. In short, bending over backwards to avoid mentioning something as obvious as race can create more problems than it solves—especially when race is relevant, diagnostic information.

Teaching our kids to avoid race at the store also teaches them to be blind to real differences in other walks of life.

So the next time your little one points out someone's skin color in public, don't shame her or him into silence. Point out that they, too, have a skin color. There are plenty of legitimate ways your kid can embarrass you in public—why let the mention of race be one of them?

Indeed, not long ago I came close to getting the opportunity to put my own advice into practice. My daughter and I wheeled up to the deli counter, and as I eyed the peppercorn turkey, she eyed the African-American couple next to us. In particular, she seemed intrigued by the husband, who must have been at least 6'6" and 250 pounds.

"Daddy, look," I heard her say. Then, with the wide-eyed enthusiasm that only the littlest of us can muster, she shouted dramatically, "He must be the biggest man in the whole world!"

While the gentleman in question was only mildly amused, Mrs. Gigantor doubled over with laughter. And I was reminded that a little honesty about what we see around us isn't the end of the world.

Racism Continues to Plague People of Color

Jerome H. Schiele and June Gary Hopps

Jerome H. Schiele is an associate dean and professor in the School of Social Work at the University of Georgia. June Gary Hopps is Thomas Parham Professor in the School of Social Work at the University of Georgia.

Writing for a special issue of Social Work *in 2009, Schiele and Hopps reflect on an earlier special issue of the journal that ran in 1982 focusing on the lives of racial minorities. The authors examine the social work profession's changing response to injustices incurred by minorities in the intervening years. In particular, Schiele and Hopps note how the social work profession both changed and benefited from 1960s civil rights movements, but they note that people of color remained vulnerable despite challenges to oppressive establishments. As nonviolent protest among minority groups gave way to civil unrest, Schiele and Hopps note, social workers' responses also became more urgent and aggressive as they moved from therapeutic approaches to helping minority groups to efforts that emphasized social justice. Today racial minorities have become more diverse and more visible. Schiele and Hopps argue that this increased visibility poses a threat to majority group members. Thus racial minority groups continue to experience social problems disproportionately to those in the majority.*

It has been 27 years [as of 2009] since the last special issue on racial minorities appeared in *Social Work*. When the issue appeared in 1982, Jerome Schiele was pursuing an undergraduate degree in sociology at Hampton University. June

Gary Hopps was editor of the 1982 special issue and had by then distinguished herself as a social work educator, scholar, and administrator. This generational difference provides an opportunity to reflect on the evolution and status of the social problems that racial minorities disproportionately experience and the response from the social work profession. Whether in the past or present, these minorities experienced and continue to experience social problems that in large part emanate from racial oppression. The social work profession's response to this form of injustice has varied over time and speaks to the specific social circumstances and challenges of a particular historical epoch.

The Earlier Issues and Problems

The 1982 special issue emerged primarily from the need to examine the profession's contributions to the debate regarding and resolution of the issue of oppression and the success or lack of success relative to its leadership. When it was published, the editor of that issue viewed the term "minority" with skepticism because of its juxtaposition with "majority" and pejorative assumption of lesser value. Problems associated with the definition of minority were addressed by several contributors outlining concerns relative to African Americans, Hispanics, and Asian Pacific Americans. Co-relatively, concerns of women were raised, recognizing the disadvantaged position of women of color in comparison with their European American counterparts who held and continue to hold [according to Hopps] "deferred power," meaning "more white women are in a socially advantageous position." Why? "Because of their individual and collective relationships to the power structure," they can use leverage that the vast majority of women and men of color can only imagine. Although their power base and potential for greater influence was obvious, no one should interpret this observation as implying that white privilege would diminish. It did not and is not only alive, but also thriving.

The 1982 special issue also emerged from questions regarding whether the social work profession benefited from the 1960s freedom struggles launched primarily by people of color. African Americans and other people of color were present, persistent, and persuasive in pressing their case for constitutionally granted political rights that were denied to them. No doubt, there were those who experienced and remembered the [Nazi] Holocaust and also shared the vision for major structural change. Because of the protests and political activities by the poor and the socially conscious, the cause for civil, human, and political rights was a priority. People of color received attention, and some rightful gains were realized. People of color were joined by other oppressed groups, such as white women, gay men and lesbians, physically and mentally challenged citizens, and new immigrants. Although the 1960s paradigm that originally advanced major structural change and enhanced corrective social justice was successful, people of color remained vulnerable relative to non-Hispanic white Americans through the 1970s and into the early 1980s.

Twenty years prior to the 1982 publication, the profession demonstrated some concern about issues relevant to people of color, then largely regarded as the "Negro problem" better known as the "black phenomenon" during the 1969 to 1975 period. In a 2007 literature review analysis of articles published from 1960 to 1975, the second editor found that at least 89 articles in *Social Work* addressed race-relevant questions, policies, and program practices. The points of discussion and presentation were derived mainly from theoretical, descriptive, and qualitative analyses. Writers were also not as representative of the populations reviewed or served. This was hardly surprising, because the number of people of color on social work faculties was very low, unless Howard University and Atlanta University (now known as Clark/Atlanta University) were included.

The social work profession also addressed the question of inequality and oppression in the 1960s. Professors and practitioners joined the oppressed, who were predominately poor urban African and Latino Americans. They were on the frontlines challenging oppressive establishments and marching with and supporting demonstrators, including those protesting the Vietnam War. The question, however, remained: Had the social work profession done enough? Was [ex-slave author, orator, and abolitionist] Frederick Douglass satisfied with President Abraham Lincoln's deliberate response to the slave system? Was [early twentieth-century black intellectual and social critic] W.E.B. Dubois pleased with [his contemporary social reformer] Jane Addams's position on suffrage for "colored people"? The goodwill of many was acknowledged and much was accomplished, but was it enough?

Social Workers Take a Look at Social Justice

Later, nonviolent civil disobedience gave way to major civil unrest, and there were calls for more urgent and aggressive change strategies. Schools of social work were challenged to assess their curriculums. What occurred was some recognition that the dominant methods [of] orientation, particularly casework and group work, did not sufficiently respond to the needs of the poor population. Therapeutic efforts, it was argued, could not or did not focus on the severe life complexities and environmental contexts that challenged poor people in their daily functioning. Inequalities in education, employment, health care, and housing, owing to long-standing political and economic disparities, were relevant to this clientele, but client empowerment, human capital, and asset development seemed not to be a significant part of the profession's dialogue, semantics, and academic or practice culture. In other words, social justice was not a working concept for the profession, and justice-based models were not promoted or used. It was the dynamics of the civil rights movement and others who used strategies of civil disobedience and urban unrest and distress that nudged, maybe even pushed, social work to expand its examination of problems from a social justice perspective.

[Then–assistant labor secretary and later senator Daniel Patrick] Moynihan's (1965) controversial report on the negro family brought even more attention to the poor population, as well as the stinging rebuttal of the report by many African American family researchers who underscored Moynihan's ethnocentrism and pathological paradigm. Thus, a new wave of strengths-based scholarship emerged in the late 1960s and throughout the 1970s to offset the overemphasis on pathology that had been used to study black and other people-of-color families. Although the focus on the strengths perspective was important, there was a tendency to deflect attention away from the critical problems that people of color continued to disproportionately confront. Moreover, the 1970s brought greater focus on the plight of other oppressed people, and social work attempted to embrace the concerns of all of these groups. However, by the early 1980s some within the profession felt that this more expansive focus on oppression drew attention away from racial oppression and how it continued to place racial minorities at risk of disproportionately experiencing the pain of injustice. The 1982 special issue emerged within this context.

Contemporary Trends and Issues

Since the publication of the 1982 special issue, racial minorities have continued to disproportionately experience social problems. From poverty to criminal incarceration rates to health disparities, the brunt of racial oppression continues to produce adverse outcomes for these groups. One of the conspicuous trends since 1982 is the greater numbers of racial minorities in the United States. In 2006, the U.S. Census Bureau reported that the racial minority population exceeded

100 million and represented about a third of the overall U.S. population. The current percentage of racial minorities represents a dramatic increase since the early 1980s, when they only represented about 17 percent of the total U.S. population. Simultaneously, the percentage of the non-Hispanic white population has diminished, as birth and immigration rates of this group have not kept pace with those of racial minorities collectively.

One implication of the growing population of racial minorities is their increased social visibility. Increased social visibility of marginalized groups has been shown to engender concerns and fears from majority groups. These concerns and fears focus on the belief that the increased numbers and visibility of racial minorities pose a threat to the sustainability of the cultural, political, and economic hegemony of majority group members. Some of these concerns and fears have translated into social policies that, among other things, have sought to end or significantly limit affirmative action, to impose English-only restrictions in public places and schools, to crack down on illegal immigration, and to impose stiffer criminal sentencing laws that mandate minimal sentences and denial of parole.

If history is our guide, the link between the population growth of racial minorities and fears over declining power and privilege among non-Hispanic white people will be unbroken. Traditions are at the heart of a group's being, and many people today decry what they view as the declining significance and prominence of white-Anglo culture as the philosophical and political foundation of America. Because the cultural values and worldviews of racial minorities frequently diverge from those of non-Hispanic whites, racial minorities continue to be marginalized and misunderstood within a society that remains reluctant to abandon its culturally hegemonic proclivities.

More Diverse and More Visible

A second implication of the growing population of racial minorities is the presence of greater diversity and difference within and across these groups. This diversity also presents unique challenges. A primary challenge is the tendency among racial oppression scholars and social work practitioners to apply the racism paradigm too loosely. Although racial minorities share experiences of marginalization that stem from white racial hegemony, these experiences vary considerably from one group to the next. The experience of workplace discrimination among Puerto Rican professionals is different from the experience of poverty and economic entrapment for many Mexican Americans who live in the Southwest. The embarrassment and stigmatization of not being able to speak English among many Asian Pacific American immigrants is different from that of African Americans who speak English but nonetheless are often racially profiled when walking into an expensive department store. Finally, the pain of intergenerational oppression experienced by many native-born racial minorities who have long-term roots in the United States is different from the more truncated and generationally specific racial injustice confronted by recent racial minority arrivals. The growing population and diversity of racial minorities essentially means that racial oppression scholars and social work practitioners must bring greater balance between identifying the shared experiences of racial oppression and emphasizing the complexity of racialized experiences.

A final implication of the increased population and visibility of racial minorities is for some to hastily assume that racism has declined in significance: that the racism of today is no match for the racism of yesteryear. People who share this belief argue that the abolition of legal racism in the 1960s opened up many new opportunities for racial minorities to gain more power and privilege in America. Increasingly so, these people contend that differential outcomes for racial mi-

norities have less to do with race and speak more to socioeco-
nomic status. Proponents of this position point to the increasing numbers and visibility of racial minority professionals,
public officials, and entertainment figures to provide evidence
to support their class-centered framework, and, by implication, to naively suggest that America has finally achieved race
neutrality. Indeed, the election of Barack Obama in 2008 as
the first African American president of the United States may
be the ultimate evidence to advance this perspective.

In America, White Neighborhoods Get Retail Services and Black Ones Do Not

Kelly Virella

Kelly Virella is a journalist specializing in investigative and literary journalism. She is the deputy editor and website content manager for the magazine and website City Limits, *and she has also written for such sites and publications as AlterNet and the St. Petersburg Times.*

In this article, Virella investigates the discrepancy in the kinds of retail services provided in Chicago's primarily black neighborhoods compared with primarily white ones. Without grocery stores and other services in walking distance, life for the residents in black areas is more difficult. Virella claims that race dictates the kinds of services available in each of these areas, and she provides evidence that suggests that when more white citizens move into black neighborhoods, the retail services follow them. Many retailers, however, claim to seek a white customer base not to discriminate against nonwhite shoppers but because their products appeal to whites. While white gentrification (the act of wealthier people buying housing property in less prosperous communities) of black communities does tend to change the retail climate, these changes often come at a price to black residents, many of whom are displaced by the process.

On the day construction workers began preparing to pour the concrete foundation for his decrepit neighborhood's

Kelly Virella, "Black and White, Seeing Red All Over: Major Retailers' Search for Green Kicks Up Racial Tension in Chicago's Gentrifying Areas," *The Chicago Reporter*, v. 38, Sept–Oct, 2009. Copyright © 2009 by Community Renewal Society. Reproduced by permission.

new Walgreens—the first new business there in more than 30 years—Ernest Gates stopped by, buoyed up about his community's future.

It was 1999, and West Haven [a Chicago neighborhood] was still more than 95 percent African American, with 54 percent of households living below the poverty level. The Near West Side neighborhood still bore physical scars of the 1968 race riots—vast stretches of abandoned storefronts and weed-choked vacant lots. But for the first time in 30 years, Gates felt, the neighborhood was on the verge of renaissance.

New, wealthier residents, many of them white, were pouring into West Haven and its vicinity to take advantage of its prime location, two miles west of the Loop. Since 1990, its white population had nearly tripled to 281, and it had shed 3,300, or one-quarter, of its African Americans. It had gained hundreds of new housing units, some selling for $300,000, and at least 2,000 more were coming. The new residents were walking their dogs after work, planting flower boxes and otherwise sprinkling the neighborhood with middle-class zest.

Now, it was getting its first pharmacy. "It gets better every year," Gates later said. "It's something we've always worked toward—to boost the demographics to a point where you start seeing a neighborhood and not a poor neighborhood."

Gates, an African-American community organizer who worked for 10 years to recruit the Walgreens, believed West Haven's growing white population would soon lure other retailers, bringing with them valuable services and jobs. The supermarket he and his neighbors needed—to alleviate their burden of traveling sometimes five miles to get groceries—would be their next target. He parked his car in front of the Walgreens construction site, at the corner of Madison and Western avenues, and listened to the din of engines, gears and pipes, confident he and his nonprofit could use West Haven's changing demographics to recruit one in the next three years. His prediction was right—and very unsettling.

Race Dictates Development

In the past 20 years, Chicago has experienced a surge in retail development in once poor and underserved black neighborhoods around downtown. At the same time, those neighborhoods have become significantly whiter, raising suspicions about retailers' motives. The whiter a neighborhood in Chicago gets, the more supermarkets it often gets, according to a *Chicago Reporter* analysis of census data and supermarket locations.

"You have to ask, what factor is driving this?" said Robert Bullard, director of the Environmental Justice Resource Center at Clark Atlanta University researching the impact of race on economic development. "A lot of it boils down to how race still dictates, in many cases, what kind of development occurs in black communities."

From 1980 through 2008, the three community areas adjacent to the Loop increased their combined white population by 41 percent, the *Reporter*'s analysis shows. Those three communities—which make up only 3.8 percent of all community areas—gained 13, or 38 percent, of the 34 supermarkets opened in communities that had more stores in 2009 than in 1980.

Two of these three gentrifying community areas—the Near West Side and the Near South Side—are still majority black by a slim margin. But most of Chicago's majority-black community areas didn't gain supermarkets, the *Reporter*'s analysis shows, and those that did either gained white population or lost black. Of the six black community areas that gained supermarkets, five have lost black population since 1980 and three have gained white population or held it constant. Over the years, the combined black population in these six community areas has declined by 84,992, or 34 percent.

Throughout the city, community areas that either gained white population or held onto their white majorities won a lion's share of new supermarkets. Of the 19 community areas that gained stores, 12, or 63 percent, fit into that category.

It's not just supermarkets. "How do you get a Starbucks to open on Canal [Street] and Roosevelt [Road]?" asked Lyneir Richardson, former vice president of urban land development for the Chicago-based General Growth Properties, the country's second largest shopping center developer until the financial crisis bankrupted it in April [2009]. "You talk about all the changes around. Look at all the condos being developed in the South Loop. Look at the prices of those condos. Look at the income level that's required to purchase those condos. Look at the education level of people who purchase these condos and look how racially diverse the community is."

"Racially diverse" is the industry's euphemism for neighborhoods with white population growth, Richardson said.

Retailers Claim to Chase Money, Not Race

The sales pitch is the same in every U.S. city connected to the global economy, including Boston; Charlotte, N.C.; New York; and Washington, D.C., said Derek Hyra, an associate professor of urban affairs and planning at Virginia Polytechnic Institute and State University researching gentrification in Chicago and other cities. Retail is growing in the urban centers in several of those cities, and so is the white population.

"There's definitely a race dynamic that plays a factor," in where retailers locate, Hyra said. "When the whites come into a community, particularly a community that's been low-income and minority, they have more income than the people who are living there. So that is a signal to retailers that there is more wealth there, and they are more likely to come when a white population moves in."

Median incomes and housing units also rose dramatically in the areas surrounding the Loop between 1980 and 2008.

The two factors account for supermarket locations as much as white population growth.

One of the supermarket chains the *Reporter* analyzed, Jewel-Osco, issued this statement explaining its decision to locate 70 percent of the stores it has opened in Chicago since 1980 in community areas that gained white population or held onto their white majorities: "Jewel-Osco considers many criteria when deciding on the construction of a new store or the remodeling of an existing facility. In fact, the company operates 184 stores across the Chicagoland area, servicing a wide range of diverse communities."

An official from another supermarket chain, Whole Foods Market, which has 80 percent of its current locations in neighborhoods gaining white population, said the chain has too few Chicago stores—only five—for the *Reporter* to conclude anything significant. Food deserts are a grave social ill but can't be cured by his stores, said Michael Bashaw, Whole Foods Market's regional president. "I think what you're asking really is a political and policy question that goes beyond Whole Foods' mission," he said. "Our mission is to promote organic food, basically, and conservation and farmland. We've never really been political about anything. . . ."

Some new urban retailers seek white customer bases, because, based on experience, that's who they believe their products appeal to most, said Frances Spencer, a retail real estate expert who for 12 years led Retail Chicago, a city-sponsored recruitment initiative. Retailers that target black, Latino or Asian markets also use race to select their locations, Spencer said. "It's really so that they can carry the product line that is most acceptable to the specific areas."

Indeed, many nonracial factors are influencing retail movement into urban areas, researchers say. For one, they contain large and underserved markets. Eight percent of the U.S. population lives in high-poverty urban areas, but only 6 percent of U.S. retail outlets, according to the Institute for Competitive Inner Cities, a Boston-based think tank. High-poverty urban areas also tend to be dense with spending power, frequently having more of it per square mile than sparsely populated suburbs. Finally, some retailers are coming to high-poverty urban areas, because, after putting so many stores in the suburbs and white urban areas, they've run out of other places to expand.

Hyra agrees that retailers chase money, not race. They're even following wealthy African Americans into historically black neighborhoods like Harlem in New York City, he said. But, historically, urban retail revitalization has primarily benefited white people, he said. It's sometimes heralded as a harbinger of racial progress, he said, but rarely is. "When you have people that live close to one another that are going to the same stores and their kids are playing with one another, that certainly is an opportunity to build racial harmony," he said. "But we typically see, as in Wicker Park, whites moving in and taking over all the public spaces and putting their own cultural values, and making the community their own as opposed to integrating the values of individuals who have lived in these communities. In the past, we have seen as white people move in, the property values raise and it makes it more difficult for a low-income minority group to stay."

Gentrification Can Displace Residents

Gates is a barrel-chested, 6-foot tall, 57-year-old, with a conservative half-inch high afro. His skin is medium brown, clear and unusually smooth, bereft of hair follicles, apart from his moustache and goatee. His brown eyes bulge from their sockets. He walks slowly and speaks in spurts of acerbic wit, sometimes with labored breath, as if it pains him to explain his views.

He has lived in West Haven throughout his life, never more than a few doorsteps away from his childhood home at Monroe and Leavitt, having been born there in 1952, when it was still one of many working-class white neighborhoods in Chicago and didn't have a distinct identity or even a name.

Rowhouses behind temporary construction fencing in the Harlem neighborhood of New York City. Gentrification often raises the cost of living in an area, effectively forcing out low-income residents. © Chris Hondros/Staff/Getty Images.

His parents were the second black family on their block—his father an entrepreneur starting a trucking company, his mother a seamstress—and witnessed white abandonment of the neighborhood within two years of their arrival.

Gates grew up to become founder and CEO [chief executive officer] of Gates Trucking—at its peak, a 40-employee company that shipped office supplies locally—but sold it in 2000, after 22 years in business, to become a community activist. Since 2007, he has been the executive director of the Near West Side Community Development Corporation, the West Haven nonprofit spearheading the community's revitalization.

When white people started returning to the community in the 1990s, the sway he believed they held with retailers angered him. "Hell yeah, I'm resentful of that" he said, about retailers' prior lack of interest. "That's a slap in the face."

But he decided that the white arrival could ultimately improve the community by exposing its poor residents to new cultures, helping them better prepare for participation in the global economy. And, after the Walgreens came, he moved ahead with his plans to leverage retailers' interests.

Gentrification won't completely displace low-income African Americans, he said. He and his neighbors booby-trapped the community against it, by interspersing low-income housing throughout. "We put scattered-site public housing in the neighborhood to make it distasteful for really, really higher income," he said. "If I've got a half-million dollar home, I don't want somebody in public housing next to me. They don't match. I can't be in my $500,000 world with Shay-Shay and Bo-Bo next door."

In 2001, when Gates and two developers he was working with to recruit the supermarket began calling Chicago grocery chains to publicize West Haven, its new Walgreens and its changing demographics, grocers weren't interested. The neighborhood was still too poor, said Glenn Azuma, one of the developers, based in Evanston. Jewel-Osco said no. Dominick's said no. Whole Foods said no. Trader Joe's said no.

But even with West Haven's high-poverty rate, officials at Ultra Foods, a Midwest-based budget grocery chain, called back with a reasonable proposal that year, in the timeframe Gates had predicted. Ultra Foods never opened the store, because, at the time, the proposed site contained a few parcels of land belonging to owners unwilling to sell. But within two or three years, West Haven's demographics became so attractive to potential supermarkets that grocers began courting Gates, Azuma and their business partner for the opportunity to lease the proposed site, now mostly owned by the City of Chicago.

Progress Comes with a Price

This spring [2009], three supermarket chains were vying for the city's approval to open a store there as early as November 2010. One stormy May evening, representatives of each grocery chain fawned over an audience of nearly 300 residents, roughly half of them white, with stump speeches and slide shows. Gates showed up too but took a back seat, blending into the audience.

"We love this site," said Chris O'Leary, a representative from Food 4 Less, a southern California-based budget grocery chain. "We want to be here. We're ready to go tomorrow, if we can."

"Pete's likes to go into food deserts and make 'em an oasis," said Charlie Poulakis, a representative from Pete's Fresh Market, a local chain known for its organic produce. "They believe this site has a lot of potential."

"We've reduced our pricing on several thousand items up to 20 percent," bragged Joseph McKeska, a representative from Jewel-Osco, a chain that for almost 20 years rejected Gates' advances. "That's our effort to get our pricing right for the community."

Most audience members applauded during the speeches. A small but vocal minority—about 10 African-American males, huddled to the left of the stage, neatly groomed, in jeans, t-shirts and baseball caps—heckled them. "We know it's gonna be an all-white community," yelled a ruddy man, with a chipped front tooth, wearing an orange t-shirt. "We know that's your plan! I ain't going nowhere!" The emcee of the meeting, one of West Haven's aldermen, Robert Fioretti, a heavily tanned blond with the wrinkles and airs of a has-been Hollywood actor, tried to placate them, before finally telling them they didn't belong.

"You either be quiet or you will be removed," he snarled, amidst audience applause.

They kept heckling, but in less than five minutes, police arrived to escort them out.

A few years after Gates and his neighbors began planning to revitalize West Haven, the Chicago Housing Authority [CHA] announced in 1999 plans to revolutionize public housing. The agency aimed, ostensibly, to reduce intergenerational poverty and welfare dependency by encouraging public housing residents to move to mixed-income communities.

About 18,000 of the city's 38,000 public housing units would be demolished, according to a 2006 *Reporter* analysis of CHA data.

The 6,000 displaced households would be offered two choices. They could rent or own a subsidized home in a new development, close to their former housing development, with market-rate renters and owners. Or they could waive their right to live in replacement housing and accept a housing choice voucher, entitling them to live anywhere in the country.

Since the agency started implementing the plan in West Haven in 2000, the neighborhood's two public housing developments have been demolished, eliminating almost 2,900 units. Some of the displaced moved into West Haven's new replacement housing. But many moved out, often into poor areas. No one can blame that on West Haven's whites, said Gates and some of his neighbors, including some former public housing residents. Most of the neighborhood's new condos aren't on former public housing sites. The vast majority were built on vacant lots demolished after the looting and burning of the 1968 riots.

For Further Discussion

1. Ralph Ellison tells *Paris Review* editors Alfred Chester and
   Vilma Howard in an interview in Chapter 1 that *Invisible
   Man* is influenced by African American folklore. He presents his "Battle Royal" sequence at the beginning of the
   novel as an example of a ritual situation culled from folklore. What other evidence of African American folklore do
   you find throughout the novel? How is the novel influenced by Ellison's passion for jazz and blues, music forms
   created by African Americans?

2. In his essay in Chapter 2, Thomas R. Whitaker argues that
   because Ellison's narrator is rendered invisible in society
   because of his blackness, others construct identities for
   him. Refer to both the article and the novel to describe
   what these different identities are and how they are constructed around racial stereotypes.

3. In Chapter 2, Christopher Z. Hobson argues that the
   Brotherhood in *Invisible Man* is an allegorical representation of the Communist Party. Other viewpoints claim that
   the novel has important ties to language and culture. Re-
   examine the novel in light of these ideas and look for
   ways in which you can contribute to these conversations
   about the novel. What other historical institutions or
   events does Ellison comment on through his work? Apart
   from music, what other cultural artifacts or events have a
   personal significance for the protagonist?

4. Randy Boyagoda argues in his essay in Chapter 2 that Ellison creates a stigmatized portrayal of immigrants in *Invisible Man*. Consider why the relationship between Ellison's
   protagonist and the immigrant characters is strained. Why
   is he at odds with these characters? Trace the narrator's

interactions with immigrants in the novel. What do his interactions with immigrant characters suggest about his own struggles as an African American? How is the plight of immigrants in America during the time of the novel both similar and unlike that of African American citizens?

5. In Chapter 3, Jerome H. Schiele and June Gary Hopps's article argues that despite social workers' new focus on social justice, racial minority groups still face racial inequality. Schiele and Hopps believe that diverse minority groups have become more visible in society and thus pose more of a threat to whites in power. Refer to *Invisible Man* and examine white characters' treatment of the narrator. To what extent is the narrator seen as a threat to those white characters? What is their response to him, and how does he, in turn, react to these sentiments?

6. Kelly Virella's article in Chapter 3 about the lack of retail services in Chicago's black neighborhoods suggests that black residents are invisible to retailers. What other examples can you think of where black people or other social minority groups go unrecognized in American culture?

For Further Reading

Maya Angelou, *I Know Why the Caged Bird Sings*. New York: Bantam, 1997.

James Baldwin, *Notes of a Native Son*. Boston: Beacon, 1984.

Edwidge Danticat, *Breath, Eyes, Memory*. New York: Vintage, 1998.

Ralph Ellison, *The Collected Essays of Ralph Ellison*. New York: Modern Library Classics, 2003.

Ralph Ellison, *"Flying Home" and Other Stories*. New York: Vintage, 1998.

Ralph Ellison, *Juneteenth*. New York: Vintage, 2000.

Lorraine Hansberry, *A Raisin in the Sun*. New York: Vintage, 2004.

Zora Neal Hurston, *Mules and Men*. New York: HarperPerennial, 2008.

Zora Neal Hurston, *Their Eyes Were Watching God*. New York: HarperPerennial, 2006.

Toni Morrison, *The Bluest Eye*. New York: Vintage, 2007.

Ntozake Shange, *Sassafrass, Cypress & Indigo*. New York: Picador, 1982.

Alice Walker, *The Color Purple*. Orlando, FL: Harcourt, 2006.

Richard Wright, *Black Boy*. New York: HarperPerennial, 2008.

Richard Wright, *Native Son*. New York: HarperPerennial, 1996.

Bibliography

Books

Robert J. Butler, ed. *The Critical Response to Ralph Ellison.* Westport, CT: Greenwood, 2000.

John F. Callahan, ed. *Ralph Ellison's "Invisible Man": A Casebook.* New York: Oxford University Press, 2004.

Robert Gooding-Williams *Look, a Negro! Philosophical Essays on Race, Culture and Politics.* New York: Routledge, 2006.

David Thomas Konig et al. *The* Dred Scott *Case: Historical and Contemporary Perspectives on Race and Law.* Athens: Ohio University Press, 2010.

Paula Denice McClain and Joseph Stewart Jr. *"Can We All Get Along?": Racial and Ethnic Minorities in American Politics.* Boulder, CO: Westview, 2010.

Alan Nadel *Invisible Criticism: Ralph Ellison and the American Canon.* Iowa City: University of Iowa Press, 1988.

Ross Posnock *The Cambridge Companion to Ralph Ellison.* New York: Cambridge University Press, 2005.

Arnold Rampersad *Ralph Ellison: A Biography.* New York: Knopf, 2007.

Shelby Steele   *White Guilt: How Blacks and Whites
                 Together Destroyed the Promise of the
                 Civil Rights Era.* New York:
                 HarperCollins, 2006.

Thomas J. Sugrue *Not Even Past: Barack Obama and the
                 Burden of Race.* Princeton, NJ:
                 Princeton University Press, 2010.

Eric J. Sundquist, *Cultural Contexts for Ralph Ellison's
ed.   "Invisible Man".* Boston: Bedford/St.
                 Martin's, 1995.

P.L. Thomas   *Reading, Learning, Teaching Ralph
                 Ellison.* New York: Peter Lang, 2008.

Periodicals

Brooke Allen   "The Visible Ralph Ellison," *New
                 Criterion*, vol. 25, no. 9, 2007.

Barbara A. Baker "Power and the Fluidity of Privilege
                 and Oppression: The Case of
                 Tuskegee and *Invisible Man*,"
                 Interdisciplinary Humanities, vol. 26,
                 no. 1, 2009.

Jean-Christophe "The Comic Book World of Ralph
Cloutier   Ellison's *Invisible Man*," *Novel: A
                 Forum on Fiction*, vol. 43, no. 2,
                 2010.

Jeff Coplon   "How Race Is Lived in America,"
                 New York Magazine, November 12,
                 2007.

Mamadi Corra   "The State of Black America on the Heels of the Election of Barack Obama as the First African American President of the United States," *Western Journal of Black Studies*, vol. 33, no. 3, 2009.

Jennifer Howard   "Ralph Ellison's Never-Ending Novel," *Chronicle of Higher Education*, vol. 56, no. 35, 2010.

Yi Jaehee   "The Politics of Exclusion: The Failure of Race-Neutral Policies in Urban America," *Journal of Sociology & Social Welfare*, vol. 37, no. 2, 2010.

Lesley Larkin   "Postwar Liberalism, Close Reading, and 'You': Ralph Ellison's *Invisible Man*," *LIT: Literature Interpretation Theory*, vol. 19, no. 3, 2008.

Julia Sun-Joo Lee   "Knucklebones and Knocking-Bones: The Accidental Trickster in Ellison's *Invisible Man*," *African American Review*, vol. 40, no. 3, 2006.

Claudia May   "The Genesis of Eden: Scriptural (Re) Translations and the (Un) Making of an Academic Eden in Ralph Ellison's *Invisible Man*," *Literature & Theology*, vol. 23, no. 4, 2009.

Reuben May and Kenneth Chaplin   "Cracking the Code: Race, Class, and Access to Nightclubs in Urban America," *Qualitative Sociology*, vol. 31, no. 1, 2008.

Radhika
Parameswaran

"Facing Barack Hussein Obama: Race, Globalization, and Transnational America," *Journal of Communication Inquiry*, vol. 33, no. 3, 2009.

Mark Peffley and
Jon Hurwitz

"Persuasion and Resistance: Race and the Death Penalty in America," *American Journal of Political Science*, vol. 51, no. 4, 2007.

Marie Timbreza

"The Cultural Politics of Slam Poetry: Race, Identity, and the Performance of Popular Verse in America," *MELUS*, vol. 35, no. 2, 2010.

Henrie Treadwell
and Marguerite
Ro

"Poverty, Race, and the Invisible Men," *American Journal of Public Health*, September 2, 2008.

Index

CPSIA information can be obtained
at www.ICGtesting.com
Printed in the USA
FFOW02n1027270214
3916FF